Stories of

Hope

from

The Women at
the Well

For everyone who needs hope…
and isn't that everyone?

Jesus answered, "Everyone who drinks this
water will be thirsty again, but whoever drinks the
water I give them will never thirst. Indeed, the water
I give them will become in them a spring of
water welling up to eternal life."

— JOHN 4:13-14 (NIV)

Stories of Hope

Introduction

The goal of The Women at the Well ministry is to meet the spiritual, mental, and emotional needs of women through connection, fellowship, and community. This inaugural edition of *Stories of Hope* brings our vision to another platform.

Since our ministry began in 2016, many women have courageously shared how the love of Jesus redeemed their lives with us. These stories were told at monthly gatherings, retreats, and conferences. They have shown us how God's redemption and grace transform broken hearts and lives into *Stories of Hope*.

It is an honor and privilege to provide a safe place where people trust us with their wounds and scars. Many of these stories have never been told before they are shared with The Women at the Well.

Through *Stories of Hope*, we pray that you will see God's grace and mercy and understand how he can take our hurt and pain and use it for his glory. We want you to know that you are seen and heard, and that redemption is a process. It's okay to be where you are, but don't give up. Our heavenly Father never gives up on us. When we surrender to Him, he is able and willing to take us farther from our pain than we can ever imagine.

We pray that you will accept Jesus' offer of living water that leads to eternal life.

– Debbie Gronner

For more information about The Women at the Well, visit **www.womenatthewell.us**

Jesus Talks With A Samaritan Woman

The Woman at the Well
— JOHN 4:1-26 (NIV)

NOW JESUS LEARNED that the Pharisees had heard that he was gaining and baptizing more disciples than John— although in fact it was not Jesus who baptized, but his disciples. So he left Judea and went back once more to Galilee.

Now he had to go through Samaria. So he came to a town in Samaria called Sychar, near the plot of ground Jacob had given to his son Joseph. Jacob's well was there, and Jesus, tired as he was from the journey, sat down by the well. It was about noon.

When a Samaritan woman came to draw water, Jesus said to her, "Will you give me a drink?" (His disciples had gone into the town to buy food.)

The Samaritan woman said to him, "You are a Jew and I am a Samaritan woman. How can you ask me for a drink?" (For Jews do not associate with Samaritans.)

Jesus answered her, "If you knew the gift of God and who it is that asks you for a drink, you would have asked him and he would have given you living water."

"Sir," the woman said, "you have nothing to draw with and the well is deep. Where can you get this living water? Are you greater than our father Jacob, who gave us the well and drank from it himself, as did also his sons and his livestock?"

Jesus answered, "Everyone who drinks this water will be thirsty again, but whoever drinks the water I give them will never thirst. Indeed, the water I give them will become in them a spring of water welling up to eternal life."

The woman said to him, "Sir, give me this water so that I won't get thirsty and have to keep coming here to draw water."

He told her, "Go, call your husband and come back."

"I have no husband," she replied.

Jesus said to her, "You are right when you say you have no husband. The fact is, you have had five husbands, and the man you now have is not your husband. What you have just said is quite true."

"Sir," the woman said, "I can see that you are a prophet. Our ancestors worshiped on this mountain, but you Jews claim that the place where we must worship is in Jerusalem." "Woman," Jesus replied, "believe me, a time is coming when you will worship the Father neither on this mountain nor in Jerusalem. You Samaritans worship what you do not know; we worship what we do know, for salvation is from the Jews. Yet a time is coming and has now come when the true worshipers will worship the Father in the Spirit and in truth, for they are the kind of worshipers the Father seeks. God is spirit, and his worshipers must worship in the Spirit and in truth."

The woman said, "I know that Messiah" (called Christ) "is coming. When he comes, he will explain everything to us."

Then Jesus declared, "I, the one speaking to you — I am he."

Give God Your Dreams

By **DEBBIE GRONNER**

"**WHAT ARE YOUR DREAMS?**" This question took me on a journey that I could never have imagined. It was 2014. I had lost my mom and my aunt (my other mother) the year before. My husband had passed away in 2009. After having cared for and lost my family members and husband, I was trying to get my life back on track.

I had been a mortgage loan officer for twenty-four years when I hired a business coach to help me build my sales. I knew of him and knew he was a Christian, which is one of the reasons I chose him. During one of our coaching calls, he asked me, "What are your dreams?"

It became an emotional time for me. I had no idea what my dreams were anymore because they had all been wrapped up in my husband. I began to explore what the desires of my heart would look like for me. As I opened my heart to the possibilities of what God wanted for me, he began to show me.

My coach suggested that I make a dream board. I had never

done that before and was a little resistant but gave in to the idea. Wow! God began to download dreams that I never thought possible. I had always imagined that I would write a book, so that went on the board. Many years ago, the Lord put on my heart that one day I would have a ministry in the community caring for others, but I had no clue as to what that would look like, so I put that on the board. There were other dreams that I had but those two were the most significant. I did, in fact, publish my book about my life journey in 2018 and it was Holy Spirit-written. Glory to God!

As God would have it, after several coaching calls, I began to hear God call me out of the business I was in to move toward a plan he had for me. It was definitely a supernatural moment—it is really hard to explain if you haven't experienced it but you just know—it's kind of like when you fall in love; you just know. The Spirit was moving in me. I felt led to resign from my job at the end of 2014 and get training to become a chaplain. I enrolled and started the training in January of 2015.

I had recently experienced hospice where my mom and my aunt had both passed away. In a strange way, I was drawn to that environment and thought that maybe that's where God wanted me—to love and care for those families and the patients in hospice. I took a faith walk and stepped into obedience to a call God had for me. I was sixty at the time and still needed income and benefits, but I said a big "yes," believing and trusting that Jesus was going to provide for me and he always has. I serve a faithful God!

I went through six months of pastoral care education and clinicals to become a certified chaplain. I thought I would just be getting training and move on to a job as a chaplain in hospice, but God had other plans. Those six months were not only for training but for healing. I was learning that in order for God to use me in the capacity that he would later reveal, I had more emotional healing to walk through.

My husband had passed away in the same hospital where I was getting my training. There was a day that the Lord placed me in the room right where my husband was when he died. I was to pray for an elderly man. God gave me a glimpse of the memory of my husband lying in the same space, and then brought me back to the man lying there. I prayed over him, walked out, and felt healed. It was hard, but so good and gracious of the Lord to care enough about me to take me there and walk me through it. He is always with us no matter what we are going through.

There were many other ways he healed me through those six months. Between my husband, my mom, and my aunt, I spent a lot of time in that hospital, so walking through those halls and loving on patients took me to all the places I had been with my loved ones. Those hard memories were replaced with memories of so many patients who were suffering and dying while spending time with their families. That was definitely hard in a different way because God had given me the humble opportunity to give back and extend the love of Jesus to hurting people. I was learning what God created me for is to love others who are broken, and to encourage, inspire, and empower them. And I loved being able to pray for them.

After six months of training, I received my chaplain certificate, and I thought I was to move right into hospice as a chaplain, but the Lord said no. So, I began moving as the Lord led, and he took me on a journey with some ladies who were transitioning to the end of their lives. What a beautiful blessing it was to hear their inmost thoughts and stories about their families! It was a privilege to be entrusted with their confidence. Still, to this day, God allows me to sit with numerous women and hear their heartbroken stories but also to witness the victory of Jesus and their redemption. God was still healing my heart through other experiences and forgiveness of some bitterness I carried in my heart. He did that through the journey I was on with some of those ladies.

I am always in awe of our sovereign God and how he knows just the right timing and what we need. We were coming to the end of 2015, and I was still listening to what God wanted me to do with all that I had just walked through. It had been quite a couple of years of listening and moving where he was leading.

Suddenly, it was like flashing billboards all around me! Everywhere I turned, I was reading and hearing about the story of the woman at the well in John 4. Jesus was telling me to start a ministry, and in prayer, he specifically said to call it "The Women at the Well." I was sobbing during that prayer and saying to Jesus, "I get it. I hear you." That was the beginning of the most incredible journey that started seven years ago. This journey has all been so supernatural because there is no way I could have done what he has called me to without the Holy Spirit's guidance. Jesus provided every step of the way throughout the last seven years in ways I could never have imagined.

Before I go into all the miracles and some of the experiences of growing a nonprofit ministry, I want to share why I believe he has called me to this with the John 4 Scripture about the woman at the well. You see, my life hasn't been perfect. (Nobody has a perfect life!) God has called an ordinary woman who has walked out a lot of suffering from her choices and what life has dealt to her.

When I was twelve years old, my only sibling and brother, who was eight years old, was tragically hit by a car and killed. That began a long life of dysfunction, partly because my family did not talk about him and, therefore, we did not grieve him. It became a secret and the big elephant in the room.

Moving forward, I fell in love at nineteen and made the choice to marry and not go to school as planned. He left me six months later, and I was traumatized. Rather than leaning on Jesus, whom I loved so much, I delved into the life my husband was living. (If I do what he does, maybe he will come back." … sick thinking.)

I was doing drugs, drinking, and being promiscuous. I then met my second husband, who would be the father of my two beautiful girls. Prior to marrying him, I got pregnant and decided to have an abortion because I was very self-centered. It was all about me and what I wanted. After the abortion, we got married and had our daughters.

We were in a fifteen-year alcoholic marriage. We had some good times in that marriage, but there was so much mental and emotional abuse of my daughters and me. I kept hanging in there, believing he was going to change, but I finally had enough.

The other issue was that I still had not engaged in my life with Jesus until the last few years of our marriage. I realized that God was the only one who was going to make our lives better, and it was time to start leaning on him. It was hard to leave because I had no idea how I would support my children and our lives because I had not worked outside the home in years. I took a faith walk and believed that God would get us through and provide for us. I believe that experience helped me to get to where I am today. He takes care of us if we surrender.

After my divorce, I ended up on my back for eight weeks with so much pain that I could not sit or walk. I had just started an all-commission job and had no benefits, so I had to wait it out and let my back heal without much medical help. God used that time to show me that I have the gift of prayer. I was on the phone praying for others. He also showed me the value of community. It takes a village, and he sent many to come and help care for my girls and me. There was even a night that my Al-Anon group brought a meeting to me. God knows our needs.

We finally sold our home and moved into something more affordable. I was so proud of that because after living in an abusive marriage, I had lost all of my confidence and didn't feel I had any value. God definitely delivered a miracle in the purchase of that home.

I had gotten back into the church and God was moving me into different groups as a leader. He was preparing me for where I am now as a leader of a nonprofit ministry organization. He had also placed me in leadership with Stephens Ministry, which was so instrumental in training me for today.

I was settling in, and after another relationship that I had surrendered, I had become content with the Lord, my children, and my career and was okay without another man in my life—forever, if that is what he willed. I had totally surrendered, and as God would have it, he provided my husband of fifteen years—my godly soulmate. We blended a family, and after a couple of years, that began to go well with God's help. Unfortunately, I lost him to a four-year cancer battle in 2009. As I moved forward through a lot of healing, I became once again content with the Lord, leaning on all of his strength and not my own. Glory to God!

I would be lying if I told you this has all been easy. It has not. There have been many ups and downs, struggles, and tears over the years, but God has sustained me. I have found so much joy in my heart that can only come from him. It's not always rosy (and he doesn't promise us that) but he does promise us that he will never leave or forsake us. We are wonderfully and fearfully made by God. He has a purpose for our lives.

Over the years, I have learned that if I keep my eyes on him, even when it's hard, I can find joy in the midst of the hard times. I have learned to wait on him, and that's not easy because I have my own agenda, but if I am quiet and focus on him in the waiting, life goes much better than forcing my needs and agenda. I am forever grateful for my sovereign God.

Because of all that I have walked through, I am so grateful for the Scripture in John 4:14, ***"But whoever drinks the water I give them will never thirst. Indeed, the water I give them will become in them a spring of water welling up to eternal life."*** *(NIV)*

Jesus gives us the living water. He is everything to me. He has promised eternity to us who believe in him—the Father, Son, and the Holy Spirit—and surrender our lives to him. He showed the woman at the well so much grace and no condemnation. That is what I believe he has asked me to do in how I treat others. All the women who come through our ministry need to be heard and seen. They need to know they are not judged but loved by Jesus and by us. None of us can earn the grace of Jesus; it is a gift from him

"Amazing Grace, how sweet the sound that saved a wretch like me!"

We launched our ministry, The Women at the Well, in 2016 and became a nonprofit in 2020. I had several women who have been in nonprofits tell me not to do it because it's hard. My response has always been that Jesus told me to do it, so it doesn't matter that it's hard. He didn't say believing in him would make it easy. I am so humbled to have stepped into this. I continue to remain obedient to what he wants from me and the ministry and how we are to make an impact on the women in the community and beyond. We are connecting women through *Stories of Hope* and meeting the spiritual, mental, and emotional needs of women through implementing programs specific to support all women.

There have been many struggles and sometimes it's just downright hard building a nonprofit organization. Sometimes I get so tired and overwhelmed, but it is so worth it when I encounter even just one woman who has been impacted by the love and grace she received. I hear confirmation after confirmation that we are doing something right. It all comes from God. He has provided so many who serve on our board, our ministry and prayer team, and volunteer in many other ways, and I am forever grateful for all that they do to further the kingdom.

God has always been a step ahead if I just wait for him to lead. He has done more than I could ever imagine with this ministry and has connected me with more women that I can count on coming alongside to help in all capacities to meet our needs. There are so many hands and feet of Jesus serving with me. God gets all the glory. We are anticipating so much more from a very big God of the impossible. I am expecting the unexpected and the unpredictable. We are seeking a space for our ministry to enable us to fulfill the vision that God has placed on my heart.

What are your dreams? Ask God to place his desires on your heart and watch him work!

"Many are the plans in a person's heart, but it is the Lord's purpose that prevails."

— PROVERBS 19:21 (NIV)

On the Other Side of Shame

By **ALICIA CARUSO**

THE FIRST TIME Debbie Gronner told me about her ministry, The Women at the Well, I got a strong nudge from God telling me that I should share my story. I didn't want to do it, but I couldn't shake the pushing from God, so I told Debbie what I was hearing from the Lord. The second time God nudged me, I heard that small voice of God say: "You haven't told your whole story." Again, I didn't want to, but God kept pushing, so here goes!

The song *Look What You've Done* by Tasha Layton tells the story of someone who is shamed by an accusing voice decrying what a mess the person has made of their life. But the song finishes with a look at what Jesus did for them. This is my song. I have allowed people in my life to shame me into not telling my whole story. But look what Jesus has done in my life! Let me tell you how He raised me up from the ashes!

After I started attending The Women at the Well meetings, a woman spoke about her childhood sexual abuse story. It gave me the courage to talk about my abuse. She started a group called Art from the Heart and used art to help us heal. The biggest takeaway for me was that I wasn't alone, that God had me in the palm of His hand.

My parents were divorced, and my Dad was an alcoholic. It was a very chaotic childhood with a lot of yelling and throwing things, but I also craved love and attention from my dad. I know I got both at times, but I always wanted more. My Dad and I had our ups and downs. When I was fifteen years old, I had my first drink of alcohol and got drunk. That same night, I lost my virginity when I was raped by someone close to me. That cycle of alcohol abuse and rape lasted for a year with that person. It was a shameful secret for a long time.

I continued to abuse alcohol when I went off to college after high school. I was raped three more times while drinking. One of those times was by two men together. One of the men was someone I had gone on a few dates with. While they were raping me, I faked hyper-ventilation in hopes they would stop. It worked, but they threw me in the shower, I guess to calm me down. Then they drove me home. All I remember next was getting in my car and speeding off to my ex-boyfriend's house. It was very late, and I didn't want to wake anyone, so I sat on their swing looking out onto their lake and cried uncontrollably. It took many years to forgive myself for something that NO ONE had the right to do to me, whether I had been drinking or not.

I don't know which came first, but I also tried to run my car into a tree. At the last moment, before I was about to hit the tree, something took the wheel and swerved the car away. I believe it was divine intervention. I had buried this memory until I took a suicide prevention and awareness seminar that The Women at the Well sponsored. I realized I was a suicide survivor when that memory came flooding back to me in the middle of the seminar, and I had to step away for a few minutes.

Soon after that, I went back to college and tried to function normally. But the day came when I couldn't keep the secrets locked up any longer, and I ended up in a psychiatric hospital in the unit reserved for the most severe cases of mental illness. My family was shocked to find out the secrets I had buried for so many years. They didn't even know that I drank.

While there, I realized that when every horrific thing happened to me, alcohol had been involved. I thought about my family history of alcoholism and called my mom, who was my best friend.

"Mom, I think I'm an alcoholic!" I said.

"Are you just trying to get closer to your dad?" she replied. That may sound like a joke, but she was very serious. She knew how desperately I wanted to be close to my dad when I was growing up.

I had to laugh, because every time I got drunk, I would cry out, "I don't want to be an alcoholic like my dad!"

I don't think anyone wants to be an alcoholic. My father had gotten sober four years earlier. When he passed away in 2020, he died with thirty-four years of sobriety. I got sober when I was twenty years old.

My mom died a year later from cancer, but she had peace knowing that I was getting my life together. The night before her funeral, I wanted a drink so bad, but I went to meet with other recovered alcoholics instead. I stayed sober only by the grace of God, but went through deep depression for years after that. I was in and out of hospitals with two rounds of shock treatment on different occasions.

At three years sober, I was hospitalized again for depression. I found out I was pregnant, and panic set in. I wanted so badly for the father to love me and want the baby, but he did not. He was just another man I used, desperately trying to make myself whole. I asked my doctor if all the anti-depressants I had been given would affect the baby, and he said they definitely would. So, I made the agonizing decision to have an abortion. Immediately after that, I had shock treatment for the depression, so some of my memories around that time have been erased.

For a year after my abortion, I quit dating. It was the first time in my life I wasn't chasing after a man to complete me. Almost exactly a year later, God brought me my husband, Jeff. On our first date, I told him about my sobriety and several of my secrets. I think I was just trying to see if he would run. Even though neither of us is perfect, he knows all my secrets now and loves me anyway.

Throughout my whole journey, God kept trying to reach me, but I ran the other way. I kept stiff-arming Jesus, saying, "What I have done is unforgivable, and I won't allow You to forgive me." I felt so lonely. After many more years of depression, I joined a church. Every Sunday, I cried, feeling so unworthy. I asked for prayers every week. I asked for prayers so often, later, one of the Bible study leaders told me she set a timer on her phone to pray for me every day. She didn't even know me, but she knew I needed prayer. I can't even say how much this meant to me!

I don't know if you will believe this or not, or think me crazy, but there was one Sunday while I was singing praises to God when Jesus appeared before me in a vision with His arms stretched wide. Instinctively, I knew He wanted me to lay my baby at His feet, and that's what I did in my heart, mind, and soul. At that moment, I released all my shame and resistance toward Jesus' forgiveness and accepted Him into my heart. With that acceptance, I was finally set free!

Every woman who has shared her abortion story or story of abuse with The Women at the Well has helped me heal. The shame that kept me silent the first time I told my story there no longer has power over me. It's taken me thirty years to be able to share my whole story.

This past year, my husband handed me a newspaper article and said, "Give it a chance."

I didn't know what he meant, but I read the article about a woman who was an abuse survivor and taught self-defense. Her organization is called Warrior Defenders. The minute I finished the article, I called her and shared a small part of my abuse story. I had always wanted to learn self-defense but knew that my PTSD from the past rapes would not allow me to learn from a man. I started taking her classes because all these years later, I still felt like a target. Even though I had some flashback nightmares during the training, I continued taking her course, and my confidence grew more and more. Eventually, the nightmares subsided.

The instructor recommended a group to me that had helped her through her recovery from abuse. I began participating in this group called Her Journey. At first, I was reluctant to delve into my past and have to feel all those feelings again. But the longer I came to the group, the more revelations I discovered about my abuse. I didn't realize that I still accepted the blame for every time I had been raped. One day after listening to me tell about my suicide attempt, a friend told me that no one deserved to be treated that way, and it wasn't my fault. She said it with such conviction and anger. At that moment, I finally felt like someone was standing up for me when all those times I had felt so alone and that no one cared. Through the faith-based classes, I have come away with even more confidence in myself, and the women in my group have become my sisters in survival.

I want to thank all of you brave, strong women for helping me on my journey to freedom. Every time I heard a Story of Hope, I felt more secure in sharing my own story. I hope that by telling my story I can give another woman the courage to start her healing journey.

I give all the glory to Jesus, who never stopped pursuing me and who saved me from the pit.

The verse that I have carried so close to my heart these past years has been: *"Be strong and courageous. Do not be afraid; do not be discouraged, for the LORD your God will be with you wherever you go." – Joshua 1:9 (NIV)*

"Be strong and courageous.
Do not be afraid; do not be discouraged,
for the LORD your God will be
with you wherever you go."
— JOSHUA 1:9 (NIV)

Resources

Families Matter Workshop
Christine Turner
(Founder of Art from the Heart)
www.familiesmatterworkshop.com

Armed Forces Mission
Lou Koon
www.intervenechallenge.org

Warrior Defenders
Holly Reese
www.warriordefenders.com

Her Journey
ARMS
(Abuse Recovery Ministry Service)
www.abuserecovery.org

Fearfully and Wonderfully Made

By **SUJEY STORTZUM**

I COME FROM a dysfunctional family, born and raised in Mexico. My mother was born in a poor, small town of three hundred people where roads were dirt and rocks, and water was limited. My grandparents were so poor that they couldn't afford to buy clothes for their kids. People gave grandma pieces of material so she could make a dress for my mom to wear. My mom had only one dress to wear, and Grandma used to wash it every night so my mom could go to school with a clean dress. Money was so tight that Mom had to quit elementary school and work in the field with Grandpa.

Mom was seventeen when she met my dad; he was eight years older than her. After dating for a few months, they got married. She got pregnant with her first child and delivered my sister by the time she turned eighteen. A year and a half later, my oldest brother, their first boy, was born.

My dad was the typical macho man. Sadly, he was also an alcoholic. He didn't provide financial support for his family. He had another family on the side, and on top of that, he was abusive. They separated after my second brother was born for about eight years. During that time, my mom had to work two jobs to be able to provide for her three children because my dad never financially supported her. With no education, her options were limited, but she was able to find a job as a maid in the house of a new missionary family that came to Mexico from the United States.

By working with them, my mom heard the gospel and gave her life to Christ. They helped her not only to grow in her faith, but they also donated clothes for my brothers and sister. She told me that one day when she was at church, she prayed to God for her life to get better financially because she didn't want her kids to grow up without education, working as slaves in the field to make just a few pesos to survive. She wanted a different life, a better destiny, for my brothers and my sister.

By that time, my grandpa started selling miscellaneous stuff in a flea market in a bigger town close to where they lived, where a dam was being built. He was doing well selling stuff to these workers and their families. My mom had the desire to start doing the same and stopped working as a maid. Grandpa gave her a tiny loan that helped her start a tiny clothing business. God had heard her prayer! She earned enough money from selling stuff on the streets to rent a small store.

The sales in that store earned her enough money to buy the store and rent the store next door! She was doing well in her business, but she was broken emotionally. After eight years, my dad came back and asked her to get together again. She loved him, and she took him back with the hopes of having a family. My dad didn't want her to get pregnant again, so she decided to see the doctor to tie her tubes. To her surprise, when she asked him for an appointment to do that, the doctor gave her the news that she was pregnant with her fourth child—me. My dad was not happy. According to my mom, my dad was hardly affectionate with her, and every time she was pregnant, he would reject her. He was rejecting her and rejecting me even before I was born.

In due time she gave birth to a chubby little girl named Perla, which means "pearl" in Spanish. In the pictures that my mom has of me when I was a baby, I never found one of my dad holding me in his arms.

When I was one year old, my mom got a strange virus that doctors in Mexico couldn't figure out. The virus paralyzed her completely to the point of only being able to move her eyes. My grandpa was desperate as the doctors told him my mom had one week to live. He decided to call the missionary couple my mom worked for years before. They were living in Arizona. They asked my grandpa to send her to the U.S. for treatment, believing God could do a miracle. She could barely speak; she was getting worse every day, so they recommended making a cassette tape saying goodbye to her children because they were sure she wasn't going to make it back. Following the recommendation, Grandpa asked her to record a message for each of us, so we could remember her after her death. That cassette still exists.

They flew her to the US, but when immigration and customs saw her, they didn't want to let her in as they also thought she was going to die within hours. The missionary was able to come to the airplane and pray for her. God told him she was going to live, so he told customs, "God told me she is not going to die." They were skeptical. He fought with all he could until he got the approval from them to get medical attention for her in the U.S. He had to sign as the person responsible for her health in case she died.

She was received in the hospital, and she could hear Spanish-speaking nurses saying, "She is not going to make it." All she could think of was her children. She didn't want to leave us alone in this world because she knew we wouldn't have support from our father. So, all she could say in her mind was, "Lord, give me the opportunity to see my children grow, to teach them about your love, and to show them you're powerful." She spent a year recovering in the U.S.

When she got back to Mexico, she wasn't able to walk and barely functioned by herself. My dad stayed with her for a few years while she recovered a little bit, but their relationship got worse and worse. He was cheating on her constantly—even bringing women to places where she would see that he was with someone else.

His drinking problems took him to the point of putting a gun to my sister's head. That was the last memory I had of him from my childhood. I was probably three or four years old. I was sleeping in my bed, and I heard my mom screaming. I ran to the living room and saw my sister, who at that time was nineteen years old, on her knees, crying, looking at my dad with hate. He was drunk, with his gun to her head, telling her, "I'm going to kill you." My mom was begging him not to kill her and to take her life instead. Years later, my sister told me the incident happened because my mom was being abused, and she had defended her.

My parents separated again and finally divorced when I was five years old. Even though he wasn't the kind of dad who would put his little girl in bed and tell her stories, I loved him with all my heart. How can you ask a five-year-old to hate her dad? I loved my dad so much that I used to cry every time he left the house to go to work. Well, one day, he hugged me, left, and never came back again. I didn't understand why he was not coming home. When he left, it was like he was dead. He never visited me or called me. Not on my birthday, not on Christmas—he was completely gone. I grew up without his presence in my life and without understanding what I could have done to make him forget about me completely, like I had never existed. I thought it was me, that I wasn't enough for him to love me. At least, that is what his silence and absence were telling me.

By the time I was a teenager, my mom was doing well economically. She had four successful stores, commercial properties, houses, etc. So, she could afford to send me to the best private schools in my hometown. One of those schools had an international exchange program with schools in different countries, so she decided to send me to the U.S. for eighth, ninth, and tenth grades in a private school in Tucson, Arizona. Being sent to study in the U.S. was not good news to me. I was a teenager, I was full of anger against my dad, and now I was feeling that my mom wanted to get rid of me by sending me far away from her just when I needed her the most.

In Tucson, I lived with the missionary family that had helped my mother, and through them, I was able to learn more about Jesus and decided to accept him as my Lord and get baptized. They helped me to grow in my faith and loved me as one of their own. After I finished tenth grade, I went back to Mexico, now strong in my faith. I got involved right away in the youth group in my church and started serving on the worship team.

When I went to college, my relationship with God started declining. I started drinking and living a non-Christian life that wasn't taking me anywhere good. In my second year at the university, I met this American guy who was in the medical school on my campus. He was seven years older than me. I fell in love with him. I thought he was the best thing that could have happened to me and decided to take my relationship to another level, which turned into a pregnancy.

When I gave him the news, I was expecting the most loving response, but he said he couldn't help me as he was married and had a little girl. I was shocked! I didn't know what to do. Once again, I felt lied to, betrayed, and rejected. He asked me not to say anything to anyone until he came up with a plan. The plan resulted in taking me to Houston to an abortion clinic. My family never knew what I did. No one knew, not even my closest friends. I was ashamed. A heavy guilt was on my shoulders, and I couldn't talk about it. One day I couldn't take it anymore, and I tried to commit suicide. My heart, my dreams, and my faith were broken, and I thought God wasn't going to ever forgive me. I thought God had forgotten about me.

My self-esteem was very low. I thought I was the ugliest person in the world and not worthy of being loved. After a year and a half, I met a professional football player. He was athletic, good-looking, educated. I couldn't believe he wanted to have a date with me! I was impressed with him. We started dating, and after a few months, he proposed in the most magical way. In my head, it was a dream! I said yes without asking anyone if this was the man I should marry.

We got married, but my dream turned into a nightmare about a month after our wedding. He started rejecting me. I couldn't believe Prince Charming was turning into a frog. Our marriage started to break. Due to his rejection, my self-esteem started going down. I thought he had another woman, and those thoughts started to kill me inside. I became depressed and felt that I was living in the same situation my mother had been in.

After four years, I confronted him about some concerning

texts I had found on his phone. He confessed to being in another relationship. After this, I decided to leave the house we shared. I told him if he wanted to work on our marriage and look for help, to come and see me. A year later, when I had not heard from him, I filed for divorce.

Making the decision to divorce was one of the hardest things I had ever done. Even when I knew everything was lost, divorce made me feel like a failure, like a loser. That's when I decided to come to Jesus again and work on my relationship with the Lord. He was the only one who could restore all the brokenness in me. Jesus helped me find peace and healing in my heart.

It took me over five years to finally consider dating again. I was still scared of marriage. A new job opportunity came to me to work for a global company based in Milwaukee, Wisconsin. That's when I met my husband. He was the guy who opened the door for me on my first day in the office. He soon became my best friend. We got married after dating for a little more than a year. The first two years of our marriage were very difficult. It was probably a mixture of different cultures, lifestyles, backgrounds, and faiths.

My relationship with God was vital for me at that time, but not so much for him. So, we did not connect well spiritually. We had a couple of miscarriages that started breaking us—first me, then him. After our second miscarriage, we were at the point of divorce. Fight after fight was exhausting. Before our third anniversary, and after our third miscarriage, we moved to Georgia. God clearly wanted us here, as I was able to find a job in two weeks. My husband was approved to work remotely the same day he requested it, and we sold our house twenty-four hours after we put it up for sale, getting full price in the middle of winter in Wisconsin! We thought this was a new beginning and a new opportunity, and it was, but our struggles continued.

I got pregnant a fourth time. I couldn't celebrate like any other mother does because the fear of losing my baby was there every day. When we passed the first trimester, we thought we had made it! We were so excited! This baby will live, we thought. Christmas arrived, and we celebrated it at my aunt's house.

Two weeks after we returned, I had my 17-week prenatal appointment. I was expecting to see the baby's sex. When she went to check the heartbeat, the nurse could not find it. She said it could be the machine because it was not the greatest technology. They sent me to a technician to confirm the baby was okay. The technician confirmed our biggest fear. The baby had no heartbeat; it was dead.

My world crashed again, falling into little pieces. I cried out to God, "Why are you doing this to me?" Why I am not sufficient to give birth?" I cried and cried. My heart was broken. The doctor asked me if I wanted to abort or if I wanted labor to be induced. Just hearing the word "abort" opened the wound in my heart and my guilt came back to me making me feel like this was happening because of what I had done fifteen years before. I asked him to induce labor. So, the next day they admitted me to the hospital.

After fifteen hours of labor pain, I felt when my baby came out. It was like someone was pulling my soul out of me. I cannot describe the pain. They asked me if I wanted to hold the baby, but I couldn't at the time. They kept it overnight just in case I wanted to see the baby the next day, and I did. I have never seen so much perfection in the size of my hand. His body was complete. His tiny little fingers, his mouth, his nose, and his eyelids were perfect. God does miracles! Seeing my baby so perfect reminded me how great our God is! In the middle of the pain, somehow, I found hope.

That's when Psalm 139:13-16 (NIV) clicked with me:

"For you created my inmost being; you knit me together in my mother's womb. I praise you because I am fearfully and wonderfully made; your works are wonderful, I know that full well. My frame was not hidden from you when I was made in the secret place, when I was woven together in the depths of the earth. Your eyes saw my unformed body; all the days ordained for me were written in your book before one of them came to be."

This verse is one of the promises that I have repeated to myself over and over for the last seven years. It took me thirty-five years to understand this verse in my life and believe what God says about me.

I saw God's amazing work in that tiny, perfect body. That's when the Holy Spirit revealed to me that I was wonderfully made, too, that he formed me for his purpose. It clicked with me that God makes no mistakes and that my life wasn't one. For years I believed the lies that I wasn't good enough, that God also rejected me. But the Holy Spirit worked in my heart through the brokenness and pain I was going through and started creating new pieces in me.

God used my pain and sorrow and turned it into something good. He gave me the strength to find joy and fulfillment even without having what I most desired—a child. I started sharing my story with other women and focused on finding purpose in the midst of my pain. God used my trials with rejection, lack of self-love, and infertility to touch other women.

Then he did what he is best at—made another miracle in me to remind me his work in my life wasn't over. After five losses, I got pregnant for the sixth time without any fertility treatment or science involved. I was so scared and didn't know if I could even rejoice, but he gave me his promise and granted my desire to have a child. Josue (JJ) is now five years old. He is a constant reminder of God's miracles in my life.

But my story doesn't end there! By God's mercy, we got pregnant again when JJ was thirteen months old, and this time not only with one child but with two! God did it again! He gave me beautiful twin boys who are now three years old.

I've seen God's mercy and faithfulness in my life over and over, and all I can do is thank Jesus! Because he chose me and created me for his glory, now I can enjoy the fruits of his mercy in my life.

The same way God worked on me, and in me, he can do in your life. I pray that as you read this story, you find hope and joy in the midst of your journey.

"For you created my inmost being;
you knit me together in my mother's womb.
I praise you because I am fearfully and wonderfully
made; your works are wonderful, I know that full well.
My frame was not hidden from you when I was made
in the secret place, when I was woven together in the depths
of the earth. Your eyes saw my unformed body; all the days ordained
for me were written in your book before one of them came to be."

—PSALM 139:13-16 (NIV)

The First Quarter of My Life

By JANET RIVERS-THOMPSON

WHEN I CLOSE MY EYES, I can see my mother laid out in an open coffin surrounded by colorful flowers at Beckett's Funeral Home in Newark, New Jersey. I can smell the fragrance of the flowers. They smelled like perfume.

My fourteen-year-old sister sat next to me in the first pew with my eleven-year-old brother and our father. I was thirteen, the middle child. My sister and I wore white dresses. Apparently, back in the day, the tradition was for children of the deceased to wear white. I don't remember what my brother wore, probably a white shirt and black pants. My father wore a black suit.

My mind was in a fog. I felt devastated, totally lost. Tears rolled down my face. This was a nightmare. Darkness seemed to be everywhere.

As the program proceeded, the soloist sang *His Eye Is On the Sparrow,* "and I know he watches me." I really did not understand what she was singing. What did a sparrow have to do with my mother? Who was he that was watching over me? When my brother, sister, and I were between the ages of seven and ten, a van picked us up along with other children, and we attended a neighborhood church to learn about God. I heard about Jesus but did not know Him for myself. My father knew about God but rarely discussed his faith with us. However, I recall him telling us that we could get baptized when we were adults because we could decide for ourselves. But I did not have a relationship with God. I did not understand the lyrics being sung as the pianist played. I cried uncontrollably.

My mother was thirty-five years old when she took her life on Memorial Day, May 28, 1963. I always thought she was thirty. We had always celebrated the holiday as a family, going to barbecue cookouts or the beach and having firecrackers and fireworks. I don't recall any fireworks the day my mother died.

At her funeral, I knew for sure that my mother was dead. My mother was gone, but where did she go? Why did she leave her family? If I had been nicer to her, would she have wanted to live? Did my mother take her life because she did not love me and could not handle my rebellious teenage attitude and behavior? Was it my fault that she did not want to live any longer? Why did she commit suicide?

I hate that word: "suicide." I've learned to use the phrase "took her life." It sounds less harsh.

After her funeral, we did not ask any questions, nor did we talk about my mother. It was as though she never existed. I slept a lot and cried a lot. I was so sad. Later, as an adult, I learned that what I had been suffering from was depression. We never received any kind of counseling. Back in the 60's, what was counseling? We were expected to continue on.

Before my mother died, our family lived with my father's

maternal aunt and her husband in a single-family home for years. Then, we moved to the brand new low-income high-rise projects in Newark, one of the largest cities in New Jersey. As children, we were excited about the move. I have fond memories of Christmas mornings and going to the beach on hot summer days, but unfortunately, I don't recall ever talking or interacting with my mother.

My mother often dressed my sister and me like twins, primarily because we were so close in age. Being a middle child, my sister was sweet and kind, and my brother got all my mother's attention. I was "Daddy's little girl" because people often commented that I looked like my father. As an adult, I realized after hearing stories from my father that my mother adored my brother. Perhaps that's why I don't recall a relationship with my mother. My brother was the "man child." He was special.

Back in the day, mothers appeared to prefer having sons over daughters. I remember reading a book in my twenties entitled *Countering the Conspiracy to Destroy Black Boys*. The author, Jawanza Kunjufu, specifically stated, "Mothers raise their daughters and love their sons." He was saying that girls were taught how to become independent by learning how to cook, clean, iron, wash clothes, etc. But mothers did all these things for their sons, resulting in them becoming grown men who were dependent on women. In some cases, the only thing boys were required to do was take out the garbage.

Reflecting on my childhood, I do not remember having a deep, affectionate relationship with my mother. I don't recall hearing my parents tell me that they loved me. I felt loved based on my primary needs being met—food, clothing, and shelter. I remember my mother registering me at my new junior high school and people thinking she was my sister. As a teenager, I was absolutely insulted. As an adult, I realized that was a major compliment to her. I often ponder how my life would have been different if my mother were still alive.

My father worked as a skycap for the New York/New Jersey Port Authority. Skycaps were men who worked at the airports carrying luggage for passengers to and from the gate. He made the bulk of his living from the tips of generous people. He worked long hours during different shifts, often leaving home several hours before his shift to deal with the unpredictable traffic driving to and through New York to John F. Kennedy Airport on Long Island.

My mother was a part-time domestic worker. She cleaned the homes of rich white folks while we were in school.

My father was an only child whose mother died when he was less than a year old and his father abandoned him. His maternal grandmother raised him until her death. Then, one of his maternal aunts and her minister husband raised him to adulthood. My mother had a large family with eleven siblings.

A couple of years before my mother died, our family moved from the low-income projects of Newark to the suburbs of East Orange into a two-and-a-half family home among people who did not look like us. Apparently, this move was extremely challenging for her. I think she felt unworthy, less than. She was out of her element. She left her relatives in the "ghetto." I wonder, as an adult, what her relatives were saying to her. The children adjusted well.

Changes! Changes! Changes!

After my mother's funeral, things changed. My father had to return to work to support his family, but he needed someone to help raise his three young children. Who could he find to take care of them while he worked long hours? A maternal aunt who lived in Philadelphia, Pennsylvania, with her daughter and family stepped in. She volunteered to live with us in New Jersey.

My aunt was very religious. She took my brother, sister, and me to a Holy Sanctified Church, which was quite a confusing experience. The preacher often shouted at the congregation. The organist and pianist played upbeat music for the choir, who sang songs that were difficult to understand and people "got happy." They "danced in the Spirit" and spoke in tongues. No one ever took the time to explain the culture of this type of church to my siblings and me, even though we spent a long time in church.

While my father worked, my aunt took care of the things around the house. She was a great cook but did not teach us how to cook or wash clothes. She taught my sister and me how to fold clothes. My brother just took out the garbage.

My siblings and I had a lot of unsupervised time. We were not adequately prepared for high school, social interactions, peer pressure, sex, or drugs. My sister conceived her first child at seventeen, one month before graduating high school. My sister had been accepted to college but decided to stay home, work, and raise her son. My father was extremely disappointed because he had programmed his three children to go to college.

I was a fearless rebel who loved my father and did not want to disappoint him by not going to college. I experimented with drugs, alcohol, and unprotected sex. Instead of keeping my pregnancy a secret when I was a senior in high school, I told my father, who decided for me to have an abortion. This was an extremely difficult moment in my life which I buried deep down within to never excavate again. I functioned like nothing ever happened and went to college as planned.

The first surrogate mother for me appeared during my junior

year in high school. She and my father took me to have the abortion. They took me shopping for clothes and everything I needed for college. She remains in my life today.

College life, being in the world on my own about four hundred miles from home, was an entirely different experience. I learned to be responsible and accountable for my behavior, which significantly impacted my development. I became a young professional with full-time employment. Graduating from college, graduate school, and post-graduate certificate programs have been major accomplishments that my father was very proud of.

However, I missed my mother.

For years, when asked about my mother and what happened to her, I would respond that she had died from a sudden heart attack. I lived with the shame of her suicidal death. I did not want to be judged or pitied. I envied the young women and men who had mothers. They appeared so happy during family gatherings, graduations, and special occasions taking family pictures. They had a mother they could talk to and share events in their lives. They could get wise counsel. I fantasized a lot about how life might have been with my mother.

When I was thirty years old, I accepted Jesus into my life. This was a life-changing milestone for me because I finally learned about repentance, unconditional love, forgiveness, grace, patience, and so many other things. God patiently waited for me to open my heart to Him. The abortions I had when I was younger, the lies and negative things I had done, were all forgiven and wiped away. I was given a clean slate to live a life following the example of Jesus.

Everything happens for a reason. Reflecting on my life, I realize that God placed several wonderful women in my path to intercede on my behalf. Losing my mother at such a young age, I learned to lie, deny, and numb my thoughts and feelings about her.

I no longer lie about my mother's death. Shame does not keep me captive to caring about what people think of me. I am blessed and highly favored. God has been so good to me. I promise to be obedient to the promptings of the Holy Spirit for the rest of my life.

Today, I've been married to a Godly man for forty years. Ironically, we married on May 28, 1983, twenty years to the day after my mother took her life. May 28 marked the end of her life but the beginning of my covenant marriage with God and my husband. We have a biological daughter who got married in December 2022.

One of the amazing things about my life is that the Holy Spirit uses me as a surrogate mother to young women whose biological mothers are "missing in action" physically, emotionally, mentally, or socially. My husband and I often have conversations with couples who are planning to get married and couples who are experiencing life's challenges.

One of my favorite scriptures comes from the book of Galatians.

"But the fruit of the Spirit
is love, joy, peace, longsuffering, kindness, goodness,
faithfulness, gentleness, self-control. Against such there is no law."

— GALATIANS 5:22-23 (NKJV)

I Was
A Good Girl

By **ARLENE MURRELL**

THIS WASN'T SUPPOSED TO BE MY STORY. You see, I was always a "good girl." I never really got into trouble growing up in the Harlem neighborhood of New York City. I was the second of seven children born to the same parents. I was the one my family considered "most likely to succeed."

As a young girl, I started my life living in the Bronx borough of New York City with my parents, siblings, grandparents, aunts, uncles, and cousins. My family always called me "the good one" and my oldest sister "the pretty one." I always thought I was a "mistake" because I didn't have the beautiful long hair my siblings had, I was not as pretty as they were and I didn't tend to follow the crowd like they did. I had a different spirit.

Occasionally, my parents took us to Goodwill Baptist Church, a small congregation a few blocks away from our apartment. It was the church my grandparents attended before my grandmother became bedridden. I absolutely loved being in church. I even served as a junior usher. I hardly ever knew what the preacher was saying because he "whooped" a lot. But being in church felt good. It felt warm, fresh, light, and different from anything I knew living in a tenement with six siblings, a dog, and a cat. But I loved it all—family, church, and a family-oriented neighborhood.

When my parents moved us from the Bronx to Harlem, we were no longer under the influence of my grandparents, so no one went to church—except me! I found a little church right across the street from the projects where we lived. Every Sunday, I got up and marched my young self over to that church and attended service. Yep, all by myself! (Hey, I think that's a song.) Anyway, I was drawn to church, and for the first time, I truly heard the name of Jesus. I am sure I "heard" it in my grandparents' church, but I didn't remember it. Later in life, I knew it was Jesus drawing me to Him. Unfortunately, it didn't last.

My family life was chaotic. My father left my uneducated, work-inexperienced mom with six children to raise on her own on welfare. With the absence of my father, my siblings went hog wild and I stopped going to church. Yet, I remained a good girl, having no desire to do the things my siblings were doing (drugs and all that). Even my friends went astray but I remained a good girl. I would later understand that Jesus had His hands on my life all along and had separated me from ALL that was going on in my Harlem environment during that time.

During the Harlem riots in the 1960s, people were looting stores, destroying businesses, and starting fires. *Not me!* I had a ringside seat. I was watching it all from our sixteenth-floor apartment window in the Grant projects in Harlem. I had no desire to do those things. Why? Because God had His hands on me, even though I didn't know it.

In my thirties, I decided that I wanted an education. Since I had dropped out of school in the 11th grade, I sat for the GED exam and passed with high scores. I realized then that I might have a chance at college. Wait…what?! That was a foreign thought because no one had ever gone to college in my family. It was a big deal to them that I would be the first. The good girl was going to college.

I started at a two-year college and did well enough to be granted a scholarship to attend a private school in Tarrytown, New York. Wait…*Where?* Remember, I was from Harlem and had never ventured outside of the four boroughs of New York. But I went and I graduated with a bachelor's degree in Nutritional Science. I then went on to earn a Master of Science in Nutrition from Winthrop College. I held positions in my career that my family could only dream of. My family was so proud of me. Now, I was not only the good one, but I was also a big shot in their eyes. I was educated and successful, had two beautiful children, and had never interacted with the law outside of a traffic ticket. Most importantly, I was a Christian.

Oh, how I wished the story ended there and we could all just close the book and go have a great day. But sadly, it was not to be. In my 50s, at the height of my career, as I was careening toward retirement, I found myself facing a legal situation that would take five years to resolve. How in the world did this happen? I was rocked to my core! Just having my name associated with a legal case was incomprehensible. Beyond belief. My family was utterly shocked, to say the least. How did the "good girl" get here?

At an office where I worked, I met an ambitious young person. We worked together for a couple of years. After this, his contract ended. He went on to establish a very successful practice and asked me to work with him as a consultant in his business. I agreed without even a mention of it to the Lord. Our verbal agreement involved his company sending me referrals for clients who needed consultation. His company would do my billing and I would also pay him for referrals..

I would like to say I was over the moon happy about this new income I was getting, but as it turned out, it was unjust gain. Little did I know he was billing the system under my credentials for work that was deceitful. Deep in my gut, I felt like something was wrong with our arrangement. On several occasions, I inquired about the legality of his process. He assured me that he had been audited on many occasions and that his process was approved by the state. However, it was not approved, and I found myself caught in a very bad legal situation that would not only take five years to resolve but would cause the greatest anxiety I have ever experienced! I can't begin to tell you the health-related problems I suffered during this time.

The sad part was that during the four months I was associated with him, the Holy Spirit was trying to warn me, but I didn't recognize that nudging. My spiritual senses had become dull. I was puffed up because of my college degrees and all the accomplishments in my career. I had stopped praying and reading my Bible. Since I had previously read the Bible, I thought I was good. I was always the type of Christian who sat as close to the front of the church as possible; but I was so far away from the Lord that before I realized it, I was sitting in the very last section of a megachurch.

One day there was a knock on my door. It was the FBI. THE FBI was coming for me, the "good girl." I felt nauseated and faint. They confiscated all my files and hit me with a subpoena to appear in court. I found out later from the judge that the gentleman had targeted me with the intent to deceitfully use my credentials and pin any negative consequences on me.

Over the next five years, while waiting for the resolution of this nightmare, I was an emotional and spiritual wreck wondering what my fate with the courts would be. Almost every night after work I sat in my living room in the dark—scared, crying, and talking to the Lord. I was so thankful that I lived alone because I needed that intense quality time with the Holy Spirit. I asked the Lord over and over how I got here. How did I go from being a Christian and a good girl to this? During this time, He showed me so many things about myself. I was blinded, FULL of pride, wise in my own eyes, self-assured, and conceited. I was blinded by the enemy and away from God, even though I was still going to church.

The Holy Spirit showed me the ugliness of pride and how and why it leads to destruction. He showed me my unforgiving heart and so much more. The enemy of my soul had crept into my heart and mind because I had allowed my relationship with God to become dull. At that time, I was no longer under His protective covering. I was still a Christian but away from Him. I had fallen so low that I was completely broken in His presence and in my own eyes. The devil had determined to sift me like wheat and to kill my witness and my flesh. The only reason I did not have a complete nervous breakdown was because God was holding me up with His grace and His victorious right hand and He had a plan for my life.

I was so sorry for how I felt I had disappointed the Lord. I repented for every transgression He revealed to me that I had committed, and I returned to Him. For five years, I spent time daily with the Holy Spirit and just Him, and my Bible. The tears

I shed during that time could fill an ocean. I was in the school of learning about myself and about Him, about forgiveness, and restoration. Where did all those tears come from? I had never cried that much (and haven't since). The Lord picked me up, healed me, and put me back on the straight and narrow path.

The Holy Spirit lovingly encouraged me with the Word of God during this time. In 2 Chronicles 20:17, He said, *"You will not need to fight in this battle."* In Joshua 1:9, He told me: *"Be strong and of good courage; do not be afraid, nor be dismayed, for the LORD your God is with you wherever you go."* And in 2 Chronicles 20:15, He said again, *"Do not be afraid or dismayed ... for the battle is not yours but God's."* (NKJV)

No matter how the court case turned out, I understood that I was washed clean in the blood of Jesus and restored by the Holy Spirit, and I vowed to go forward, tell the truth in court, and face the consequences. I was still somewhat scared but I was trusting God to be with me and to defend me.

I saw God's hand in my situation all the way through the ordeal. The prosecution asked me to be a witness for them against the young man. I committed to telling the truth regardless of who asked the questions and regardless of the outcome. God had softened my fears and by the time the case came to court, I was strong in Him.

During the court session, the Holy Spirit reminded me that I did not need to fight in this battle, and so as much as I wanted to, I did not defend myself in any way at all. I left it up to the Holy Spirit to defend me with the truth. That's when the judge told me that I had been targeted by the young man because he had told his staff that he was looking for a little old lady with state credentials to partner with.

In the end, God worked everything out for my good. He caused the judge to see the truth and I was vindicated. Unfortunately, the young man received time in federal prison. While I am not happy this happened to me (nor do I rejoice that the young man will have to spend time in prison), I am so grateful for the lessons I learned on this journey and the fact that this brought me closer to the Lord.

If I were to give advice to anyone, especially Christians who may think that they cannot fall or be deceived by our enemy, I would say:

Never stop reading your Bible. Never stop praying. Always acknowledge Him in ALL your decisions. Pay attention to the nudging of the Holy Spirit. Beware of wolves in sheep's clothing. Stay very close to the Lord.

Love the Lord your God with all your heart, soul, mind, and strength for real, and lean not on your own understanding. *"Trust in the LORD with all your heart …. In all your ways acknowledge him, and he shall direct your paths."* (Proverbs 3:5-6) (NKJV) *Be intentional about letting the Holy Spirit of God lead you continually!* (Galatians 5:16-18). He will perfect that which concerns us. (Psalm 138:8).

Most importantly, if you fall, know that there's forgiveness in Jesus. He will pick you up, dust you off, and give you a fresh start. To God be all glory, honor, and praise!

By the way, I dropped the "good girl" title. I am a sinner like you and everyone else—saved, delivered, and set free by His grace!

May you be blessed and helped by this testimony.

"No one is good
but One, that is, God."
— MARK 10:18 (NKJV)

Doing Hard Things

By **TRACEY BROOKS**

CHANGE IS HARD. That's why it took five years for me to leave an abusive situation.

At some point in life, we have all come through something that was hard to do. Whether the hard thing was a choice or not, we did it. And most of us have said to ourselves after it was over, "Whew! I'm glad that's done!" and "Wow! I feel stronger having gone through that!" For most of us, this last thought doesn't come to us until we are happily on the other side of the horrible events. At least that's true for me, because I didn't think I could make it while I was in the throws of it.

I left a relationship hoping for a life of peace and joy, and although I didn't have to endure the verbal and physical abuse any longer, I did not gain instant the peace or joy I was seeking. Instead, I found myself homeless with two children staying in a pay-by-the-week hotel surrounded by people from different backgrounds with an air of hopelessness looming. In order to keep me and my children from being sucked into the vortex, I kept my children close, reading the word of God, believing that any day now I would acquire a good paying job to sustain us and that God was going to show us the way to our own home. I just didn't expect how long it would take and all that awaited us on the journey.

MAKING THE TRANSITION

When we decide to change is when change begins, and the transition is painful and hard. I imagine the pains of change can be like what a drug addict experiences once they commit to becoming drug-free. Although I was sure I was on the right path, it was like the beginning of a boxing match when you were told that you would surely win the fight, but the first punch in your face knocks you to the ground and your nose is bleeding. Doubt says, "You really think you are going to win this fight?" while your face is throbbing in pain and the room is spinning. This is when you must believe beyond what you can see or feel.

"Get up! Get up!"

You hear this voice coming from the depth of your spirit.

"You are a victor, not a victim!"

So you stumble to your feet and keep swinging wildly because you cannot see straight.

This is how the transition to victory feels. Many times it's a mental fight, believing and trusting the process.

AFRAID, BUT YOU MUST KEEP GOING

It is not easy.

I imagine the people wandering in the wilderness for forty years did not know that their journey was technically only a forty-day trek. We, too, alternate between not trusting God and believing that no matter how long it takes, it's all in his plan to get us to a better place mentally and physically. Yes, I had my days where I felt like it would be better to be back in the situation I left. Thankfully, this thought only came when things got really rough and dark. There were many times when keeping the faith was very hard, but that is when I would cry out to God after the girls were asleep. I would cry hard with my hands over my mouth so I would not wake my daughters. And after the hard cry, I would pray, begging God for strength to keep trusting that he is with us.

On the weekends, early in the morning, my girls and I would do our laundry. While waiting in the parking lot outside the laundry room, we would jump rope and do exercises before the others in the hotel woke up. This was the best time of the week to avoid some pretty scary characters. On Friday and Saturday nights, we could hear all the activities outside our door, but early Saturday or Sunday morning, practically no one would be out and about at the hotel.

I remember a particular morning after the night of the hard cry, my daughter was jumping rope, and she casually said, "We will be out of here soon." I quickly high-fived her and asked what made her say that.

"I just feel it," she said.

Within two weeks, we were able to move to a place of our own, a place that gave us eighteen months rent-free! God is good!

Doing hard things is really about choosing what you believe is the best thing to do, even when you are afraid.

The day I left with my children, I grabbed the backpack and told the girls, "We are leaving. Grab your stuff and come on!"

It was chaotic. My heart was racing, but I had heard a voice on the inside saying. "If you stay, it's only going to get worse."

That day, I felt the strength to jump, but it was as if I had scooted to the edge of the plane with a parachute that I did not know how to work. It was an emergency, and the plane was on fire. I had no choice.

People, this was so intense for me. For a girl who is afraid of heights, it was scary! On that day, I had the strength and an inner knowing that God was with me. It's crazy to think that you can be trusting God and still feel fear, but it's the truth of my experience.

Shadrach, Meshach, and Abednego may have appeared cool and calm on the outside, but when they first heard they were being sent to the fiery furnace, I imagine they were gripped with fear. (Daniel 3:16-28)

As believers, when we are faced with hard things, we know that no matter what, God is in control. I quoted Jeremiah 29:11 often to strengthen my mental and emotional muscles in the truth of God's word. *"For I know the thoughts that I think toward you, says the Lord, thoughts of peace and not of evil, to give you a future and a hope."* – Jeremiah 29:11 (NKJV)

Reading the word of God regularly was my saving grace. When my bank account looked like I had no way out, God's word gave me hope. Although I had read and heard the story of Shadrach, Meshach, and Abednego preached several times, reading it during this juncture gave me strength and a resolve I had never known before. Although these Hebrew boys weren't sure what their fate would be, they chose to believe that God was aware of the situation and that He knew what would be the best outcome. In Daniel 3:18, the boys told the king that even if God did not save them, *"We will not serve your gods."* That is a clear example of doing hard things.

Our testimonies aren't testimonies until we pass the trusting God test. Faith is believing while we don't understand and don't know the outcome.

When things got tough, my faith muscles grew stronger. We have to believe that on the other side of difficulty, there is something better for us than whatever we have now. Whatever we have to endure to get to it is worth it.

When we experience failure, we can choose to become better or bitter. I've learned that when I choose to become better, it helps me to find the lesson in the pile of mess. It helps me see the bud of growth.

I think of the scripture in Matthew 7, *"Seek, and you will find…"* On my journey, I had to continue to remind myself that I truly believe that God has my best interest in mind, that he has plans to give me hope and a future, as he promises in Jeremiah, no matter what I am going through. During some of my most challenging times, I would have these conversations with my Lord and tell him my true feelings about the current situation. One of these conversations, in particular, was when I had been going to every church service that was available, but I could not shake feeling so lonely. I mean, I was low. I had people I could talk to, but nothing was taking away my sense of deep despair. I was crying out to God nightly in my prayers, and the next morning I would put on my smiling face and get the girls up and off to school.

I had begun working two jobs, but a new manager on my first job did not want to allow me to do a split shift so that I could pick up my daughters from school and take them back to the hotel. I told my manager at the salon where I was working about the situation, and she said she would be able to give me more hours. So I gave my two-week notice, and they let me go that week. I felt that my life was still spiraling down. Every time I thought I should be at the bottom, something else began to feel unstable.

CRYING IN MY CAR

On my hard journey, I remember the one and only time I was let go from a job. After I gathered all my things and got into my car, I just sat there, thinking, I was not let go... I just got fired. Wow. I just got fired."

And then I said to myself, "Shouldn't I be crying right now? I mean, I did need this job, but no tears would come. This was significant for me because I was normally a "crier." I cried with people when they cried. I cried when I was angry. I cried tears of joy—I mean, I was a crier. But I had just been fired, and I was sitting in my car, not crying. Wow.

I knew something new was happening for me because I began to praise God for whatever He was about to do next I did not know what that would be, but I felt a new level of trust in God. At that moment, I understood what joy really was. I looked over how I had conducted myself on the job and realized I had given the best I could give, and I was okay with the outcome.

We all desire a place in time where we are able to rest and experience a life of ease, no disturbances or disruptions, the comfort zone. The comfort zone feels great for a time, but after a while, it is where we start to decay. In nature, when things are stagnant, they die. I see this in the changing of the seasons. If the seasons don't change, we experience extremes. When we have beautiful sunshine for too many days without rain, things dry up, wither, and die. When we have too many rainy days, things wash away. They don't root and grow. What I've learned is that when we don't experience any challenges, we, too, wither mentally.

I experience joy as a deep inner peace, a trusting that it (whatever it is) will work out just as it is supposed to, when it is supposed to, no matter what is happening in my life. Now, when fear creeps in and I am aware of it, I ask God to help me to have courage although the situation becomes difficult.

LIFE LESSONS

To truly live to our fullest capacity is to live courageously. I believe God is omnipresent and trust him to guide the life that he designed for me. There are so many biblical examples of how God uses all things to work out for our good and his glory. Perspective shifts and a lot of forgiveness are keys to overcoming life's challenges.

My faith and belief in God grow stronger by overcoming the obstacles on my life journey. Scripture says that we overcome by the word of our testimony, and sharing mine is how I help to encourage others that whatever they are going through, they can make it. They can come through it a better person. Now that I am out of that situation, I can say that I have grown immensely. I look back and see how I allowed fear to hold me captive, fear of being embarrassed, fear of people thinking less of me and believing that I couldn't raise the girls alone.

The scriptures say that all things work together for the good of those that love God and that are called according to his purpose. In Genesis 50:20, Joseph says to his brothers: ***"You intended to harm me, but God intended it for good to accomplish what is now being done, the saving of many lives."*** (NIV)

When I look back over my life, I see God's hand guiding me through.

"You intended to harm me,
but God intended it for good to accomplish
what is now being done, the saving of many lives."

— GENESIS 50:20 (NIV)

Miracles
of God

By **CATHERINE ALBEANESE**

LIKE MANY OF US, I was born into a toxic dysfunctional family. My parents and my paternal grandparents lived with us and I had a brother who was seven years older than me. On the outside, we appeared to be the *Leave it to Beaver* household. I had extravagant birthday parties, elaborate vacations, and anything a child could want. We did all of the things other families did but, behind closed doors was another story.

My childhood was filled with physical, emotional, and sexual abuse. It was a roller-coaster existence. There were highs and lows and instability all around me. I tried to protect myself, but when you're a child you have trouble putting up boundaries and expressing what's going on inside of you. I learned how to check out when the stress became too much. My family functioned from crisis to crisis. Nothing was normal, and I didn't know what normal was.

As I got older, I had no goals, no hope, no dreams. I felt like any spark I had inside of me had died. I was empty and numb. I lived in survival mode because that's all I knew. I felt if something didn't change, I didn't want to be here anymore. I was exhausted from living, and that if this was life, I was ready to end it.

My brother had a neighbor whom I had spoken to casually in passing. One day she asked me if I would be interested in going to a Bible study with her. At that point in my life, I was married and had gone from the frying pan into the fire - the cycle was repeating itself. When she invited me, I thought, "Why not? I've tried everything else."

That was the beginning of my life being totally changed.

The people I met there were kind and loving and seemed to genuinely care about each other. That's where I met Jesus. I had heard about Jesus, but He seemed so far away and unreachable. He was up in the sky somewhere. There was no relationship with Him. I prayed because that's what you do, but I never expected Him to answer. I formed a close bond with some of the women and began to trust again. I learned who He was. I learned how much He really loves us and is interested in every detail of our lives. The big things and the insignificant ones. It was there that I started to have a ray of hope. During this time, my marriage began to crumble. I was six months pregnant and things were so out of control I had no choice but to leave. That's when I began to see Jesus do miracles.

The day I decided to leave I waited for my husband to go to work and then called everyone I knew to help me. I was packed and out of the house in six hours. While packing, I began calling storage houses, and every one that I called would say they had no vacancies. I began praying. The last place I called started to say no vacancy, and I quickly told her my predicament. The woman on the phone said, "I have a waiting list. Come now, and I will take you." This was the first miracle He did for me, but many more followed.

Later that night, I flew to Atlanta, Georgia, to stay with a friend for a few months to figure out what I was going to do.

My family knew what had happened, and my mother told me to come back and live with her. We got an apartment in subsidized housing. We had no phone. One day I said to the Lord, "I think I need a phone. What if I go into labor and I'm alone I would need to call someone?"

He told me to go to the phone company.

"They want a $100 deposit, and I don't have it," I told him. But then I said, "Alright, I'll humiliate myself if that's what you want," and I went to the phone company. This lady came up to me and asked if she could help me. I didn't answer her. I felt two hands on my back. I sidestepped her, walked straight to the back of the store, and stood there. Another lady walked up and asked the same question.

I looked at her and said, "As you can see, I'm about to give birth and I need a phone."

"Don't I know you?" she asked. "Did you work at the phone company in Metairie?"

It had been thirteen years ago and I had completely forgotten about that.

"Yes," I told her.

She went behind the counter and handed me a phone and said she would have it turned on that day. I was stunned. There was no mention of a deposit. That day I learned how He works all things for your good.

I went into labor a few days later. My daughter was born but was very sick. I had developed an infection, and we were both septic. The Lord was so close to me. His spirit rested on me. She was kept in the intensive care unit for ten days before I could take her home. I never knew love until I looked into the face of my daughter.

I was happy when I was able to return to the Bible study. I got so much love and encouragement there. I had missed our times of praying together and the true joy of being with people who genuinely cared about you. There was one lady in particular, Mary, who I really trusted. One day while in her kitchen, my life story began to pour out of me. I felt like I was on the outside of myself telling her everything I had gone through. I tried to stop but couldn't. I had told myself no one would ever know about my life. I hadn't even told my husband. The secrets were locked deep inside and were never meant to come into the light. That day was the beginning of Jesus healing me. I had a long way to go, but it was a start.

Every time we got together to pray, the ladies would say, "I see a nurse's hat on you." I told them I would never go back to school. Then one morning while praying, I had a vision. I was out in space and saw the world turning ever so slowly. It was beautiful. Then I heard the Lord say, "What if I had told the Father no? What if I had not come to save you?"

I began to cry and told Him I wasn't going to be saving people.

"Don't you remember how much trouble I had in school?" I told Him. "Face it, I'm stupid. I could never accomplish that."

"And what about Amanda? How will I support her? How will I do all of this? It's too much! I don't have any money!"

I thought more about it when I got home. I called the state hospital to find out what programs they had and found out they had a one-year training program to be a surgical technician. I thought, "One year? I could maybe do that. It's only a year and they pay a stipend, which would be a big help."

That night, my friend Mary called and gave me a word from the Lord. It confirmed all that the Lord had been speaking to me:

"Don't worry about money or Amanda. They will be taken care of by my Spirit," she relayed to me

One year later, I graduated. It was a grueling program, but I made it and was able to get a good-paying job. I started thinking that if I could do this, I'd try nursing school. Again, the Lord came through for me with the help of my prayer warriors. It took me five years to complete nursing school.

During this time, my mother and I were having problems. She was becoming increasingly controlling and argumentative, and I felt like my life was being sucked out of me. I decided it was time for me to leave and get my own apartment. I happened to read Ezekiel 12, which told me exactly what to do. I rented an apartment a few blocks from my daughter's school. It was October 31, 1989. I was terrified of having to tell my mother we were moving, but I knew I would die if I didn't leave.

November came, and I told the Lord, "I can't tell them now because it's Thanksgiving." Then Christmas came and went. On the first day of January, my daughter and I were both sick with the flu. I told my daughter to go and take a bath. While my daughter was in the bath, I told my mother we were leaving.

"God told me to leave and that we are moving the next weekend," I said.

She began yelling and screaming.

"So, your God told you this? What kind of God do you serve?" she yelled.

That's when I got my daughter and left for the apartment. I

waited until I knew she was in bed before we went back. My family was furious with me. No one would help us move, so my daughter and I carried our things out by ourselves, and I hired three men to get the furniture. The day we moved in, I told her not to unpack much because I didn't think we would be there long. That was in January. By May, we were on our way to Georgia.

The day my daughter got out of school that year, I got her report card, hired three men to load a truck, had a girlfriend drive the truck, and we drove my car. I had transferred to Georgia from my job in Louisiana but only knew one person there, my ex-mother-in-law. I had no one in Georgia to help me unload. I didn't know how the two of us would unload this truck.

I began to pray and call on Jesus for help. Feeling overwhelmed, crying, and praying, we got to the apartment I had rented and opened the back of the truck. I handed my daughter a box, and I took one, and we walked into the apartment. When we walked out there were three men standing on the side of the truck. They had on blue jeans, work boots, and no shirts.. One asked, "What are you doing?"

"We are trying to unload this truck," I said.

"We'll do it for you," another one said.

We looked at each other.

"Okay," I said. I tried to talk to them and asked where they were from.

"Around here," one answered.

They just kept working and not talking. I remember thinking how strange they were. Then I went into the apartment to get money to pay them and when I went outside, they were gone. I was looking for them when my daughter said, "Mommy, those were angels."

"You knew?" I said, shocked.

"Yes, I thought you knew," she said.

The Lord has been so faithful to us. He took me from living in the projects and gave me a profession, a home, and a blessed life. He literally saved me from a life of despair and hopelessness that was torn and fragmented. He is and always will be someone you can trust no matter how desperate and hopeless your situation is. You can always call on Him as He is much closer than you could ever imagine. The worse the situation, the stronger His love and presence are with you. There were times I felt like He was literally physically carrying me.

When you feel like you can't go on, open your heart and ask Him to come, and forgive you and give Him your life. He will love you, help you, change you, and give you a whole new life if you just trust Him.

"Here's what I've learned through it all.
Don't give up; don't be impatient;
be entwined as one with the Lord.
Be brave and courageous, and never lose hope.
Yes, keep on waiting—for He will
never disappoint you!"

—PSALM 27:14 (TPT)

From Broken to Beautiful

By **LIZ JAKWAY**

REDEMPTION IS A POWERFUL WORD. It speaks of a redeemer, of a selfless heroic act that saves someone from imminent danger. The hero in my story—the Redeemer—is Jesus Christ, the Son of God.

Long before I knew Jesus, I knew God and prayed to Him. As a young child, I went to Catholic church with my family. I believed in God and heard that Jesus died on the cross. I saw the statues of Him in church but didn't know He died for me so my sins could be forgiven or that He rose from the dead so I could spend eternity with Him in heaven. In church, I only saw the crucified Christ.

My parents divorced when I was five. My mother, my four siblings, and I moved in with my grandparents. My mother only stayed a short time because she and my grandmother didn't get along. They agreed that my mother should leave. I didn't see her again for two years. I missed my mother terribly and cried myself to sleep every night.

That tender, vulnerable heart is what my grandfather took

advantage of, telling me I was special to him. For four years, he molested me. When I was nine, I found the courage to tell him what he was doing was wrong, and I asked him to stop touching me. He complied. I didn't tell anyone about it until I was thirty.

My father was a bad man. Among other things, he was a con man: charming but deceitful. The only thing I remember about him was his smile. My mother never spoke of him, and my grandparents feared for our safety. In an effort to protect us, my grandparents adopted us and changed our names.

I came home from school one day when I was twelve, and my grandparents told me my father had been murdered. His body was found in a submerged car. This didn't surprise them, but I had trouble accepting that he was gone. I had nightmares, dreaming he would come walking up out of the water.

That was the year I also made a vow to never be like my family. By that time, my mother, my father, and my siblings had been in trouble with the law. That was not who I was or the life that I wanted. I put the troubled parts of my childhood behind me, becoming confident and independent. I won spelling bees, had perfect attendance, and was presented with a trophy for having the highest GPA ever in my school. I had dreams. I was going to do something with my life. I liked helping people and wanted to become a teacher or a policewoman. I wanted to make a difference in the world.

By the time I was fourteen, one of my brothers was a drug dealer, the other was in reform school, and my older sister had a baby and got married. My older brother and my younger sister were the only ones who received my grandmother's love. Unless I did something extraordinary, I was invisible. I achieved so much in elementary school, but everything was harder in junior high. My brother relentlessly tried to make me do drugs so that I wouldn't tell on him. I grew so tired of having to fight to be somebody and to be loved. Eventually, I gave in to his pressure, leaving me feeling hopeless. I decided I would run away from home. Who would miss me? I left my grandmother's home and never returned. I went to find my mom, but that was a mistake. I didn't fit into her life. Not knowing what else to do, I contacted my sister's old probation officer, who helped me find a place to stay.

When I was fifteen, I went back to my mom. She agreed to let me live with her and her boyfriend. My mother worked nights, and it wasn't long before her boyfriend raped and threatened me repeatedly. When I found the courage to tell my mom, she didn't believe me. When his son caught him attacking me, she had to face the truth. Shockingly, she chose her boyfriend and told me I had to leave. What did I do wrong? How could she turn me away? I was only fifteen!

I called my old friend again, and she found me another place to stay. There is such a thing as too much freedom. I was fifteen, renting a room that my grandmother paid for from a woman who took in boarders. I could do whatever I wanted as long as I went to school and was home in the evenings. My friends and I hitchhiked all over town, even at night, with no fear. I had been smoking marijuana since I was fourteen but now started using other drugs.

My grandmother was hospitalized when I was sixteen. I visited her and promised I would move back to help care for her, but she died two weeks later. I was devastated. It was like losing my mom. After her funeral, I told my mother's boyfriend I wanted to go home with my mother, but only if he promised never to touch me again. He complied.

The summer before my senior year of high school, I got my own apartment. I went to school in the morning and worked at the county employment agency in the afternoon. I was young, I was free, and again, could do whatever I wanted. I started drinking and did every drug imaginable except heroin. There was no way I was sticking a needle in my body!

Two years later, I got pregnant. Friends encouraged me to get an abortion, but I couldn't. I didn't know what to do. I quit my job as a bartender, quit college, and didn't even have a car. I stopped doing drugs but kept smoking cigarettes and marijuana. I only saw a doctor once when I was eight months pregnant, yet miraculously was blessed with a beautiful, healthy baby girl.

I bounced around from family to friends and from job to job until I was able to go back to college and get my own place. The following year, I met a guy who was a little older than me. I thought he was wonderful and wise, but I was wrong! We lived together, but he wasn't good for me or good to me. Why do we choose the bad guys? I started drinking again and became addicted to cocaine.

The only good thing in my life, the most important thing to me, was my daughter and the joy she brought me. Her babysitters and preschool and kindergarten teachers were Christians, yet they never judged me. She had this wild, crazy mother, but she was protected by God long before I realized it. She fell in love with Jesus when she was three, always singing cute little Jesus songs.

In the car when she was four, she said, "Momma, I can't wait to die and go to heaven and be with Jesus." I slammed on the brakes and said, "What did you say?" She repeated it. Great fear overtook me, and I told her never to say that again.

My heart was restless. Why would a four-year-old want to die? What was it about this Jesus? What Saint Augustine said is true, "You have made us for Yourself, O Lord, and our heart is restless until it rests in You."

I started talking to my older sister, who I knew had become a Christian. I called her one day, and after work one Saturday night, I drove fourteen hours to her church to give my life to Christ. My sister and her pastor's wife bought me a Bible and taught me from the Scriptures for two days, developing a deep reverence for the Word of God in me that is still evident thirty-nine years later.

I stopped drinking and using drugs, but three weeks later, friends I used to party with spent the night. I wrestled all day with what to do, eventually giving in and partying with them. I was the last one awake that night. When I walked into my bedroom, the room kept getting darker and darker. As I lay down, I heard the audible voice of God, "This is what it's like in the darkness. You choose whether you want to stay in the darkness or live with Me in the light." I chose God and surrendered my life completely to Jesus that night.

Jesus is the hero of my story. He is the one who redeemed me. I was helpless and hopeless until He stepped in and showed me who He was. He is my Redeemer, my Savior, my Protector, my Provider. His faithful love has been my anchor and my only hope.

Jesus changed my life and gave me the courage to no longer be a victim. Yes, many things were done to me, but there were also choices I made that I was responsible for. Most women are strong, not because they want to be, but because they have to be. I didn't overcome any of this in my own strength. I found courage and rest in God's strength. Because He created me, He knows what is best for me. I truly love Him, and like the air I breathe, I need Him every day. The truth is, I am not good on my own—none of us are—but God can be trusted in the driver's seat.

Although there are things we will never understand, walking by faith and not by sight allows God to capture our tears in a bottle and redeem them (2 Corinthians 5:7; Psalm 56:8; Revelation 21:4). God had to walk me through a lot of forgiveness, even for myself, which can be a process. Sometimes the pain is so incredibly deep that our hearts and minds cannot release it until years later.

Two years after I became a Christian, I drove out of my neighborhood and saw my mom's old boyfriend's car at the bar I used to work at. I felt the Holy Spirit nudging me to go in and talk to him. I refused. Why him? Why now? I hadn't been back to that bar in years. I had a new life and no desire to go in there. Throughout the day, the Holy Spirit kept nudging me. Finally, I told God if his car was still there, I would stop. It was.

I walked in to find him sitting at the bar. I said hello and asked if he would sit at a table so we could talk. He complied. I told him I forgave him for everything he had done to me. I told him Jesus loves him, and I love him too. Tears rolled down his face. I hugged him, said goodbye, and never saw him again. Although I resisted initially, that act of obedience released me and released him. I was no longer consumed with negative thoughts about him and rested in God's perfect peace.

The same thing happened with my grandfather about ten years ago. Driving in my car, I saw an old El Camino. It reminded me of when my grandfather was sick and dying of cancer. My brother drove him to chemo treatments in downtown Miami in the back of an El Camino. He sat in a wooden chair, and my younger sister and I rode with him to keep him safe. I had no sympathy for him. But now, years later, God reached down and touched something deep within my heart, and I thought about how scared he was.

I reflected on how I always thought he deserved that grueling cancer, but now couldn't stop thinking about his fear. God pierced my heart. I forgave my grandfather and asked God to forgive me for my hatred toward him. Peace came flooding in.

Five years ago, God moved again—this time with my father. One night, I did an Internet search on his murder while doing some ancestry research. My grandparents believed he had been murdered by the mafia in Miami Beach. Much to my horror, a newspaper article with a photograph of a car popped up, talking about his bullet-riddled body. I threw my laptop down and walked away for a few days.

When I went back and read the article, I was furious. It revealed another layer of just how evil my father was. He was murdered in a gunfight over who would become the next leader of the local KKK. How could he have such hate in his heart?

I couldn't sleep that night. The next morning, I was going to a friend's father's funeral. I cried the entire thirty-minute drive. How could he be so evil? How could he be my father? I pulled into the church parking lot and sat for a few minutes. Still overwhelmed, I sent a text to a few friends asking for prayer. I was really struggling as I walked into the church. Toward the end of the service, they offered communion. I knew I couldn't receive it with what was going on in my heart.

I cried out to God, literally in tears, and asked Him, "What is this? Is it grief?" He spoke to my heart and said, "No, Elizabeth, this is not about grief. You have been grieving your father your entire life. This is about forgiveness." I was blindsided and told God He would have to give me time. He spoke again and said, "I don't want you to carry this another day." In my pew, I chose to obey God and forgive my father. Then I took communion. When I got back to my seat, I knelt, weeping, and asked God to forgive me for my feelings toward my father. Perfect peace followed. In my heart, I buried my father, too, that day.

Life is a bumpy road. I can't say I would do it all again, but am grateful that God has been with me, even when I couldn't hear His voice or feel His presence. I am blessed. I have a beautiful family. I have a business that provides what I need and allows me great freedom. I have tremendous opportunities for ministry—sharing the gospel and following my passion to teach women the Word of God.

"For God so loved the world that he gave his one and only Son, that whoever believes in him shall not perish but have eternal life." (John 3:16). (NIV)

Jesus died for you, and He died for me. If you've never surrendered your life to Jesus and allowed Him to take all of the hurt, all of the pain, all of the guilt, and all of the shame, I encourage you to stop where you are and cry out to Him. Ask for His forgiveness. Surrender your life to Him and allow His love, grace, and peace to wash over you. He will give you new life—eternal life—in Him.

If we can let go of our pain and surrender it to God, He can turn it into a testimony of His incredible power. He takes the broken pieces of our lives and creates beautiful stories of redemption, allowing us to connect with others, and comfort them in their pain (2 Corinthians 1:3-5). Don't be afraid to share your story. It may encourage someone and give them hope.

"You keep track of all my sorrows.
You have collected all my tears in your bottle.
You have recorded each one in your book."
— PSALM 56:8 (NLT)

I'm Worth Saving And So Are You

By JANET MYKING OTTO

ONE COLD, WINTER NIGHT in a small town in northern Minnesota, there was a rap at the door. I'll never forget his voice or the news he delivered: "Bern is gone—he died tonight."

Our family pastor had entered through our kitchen and into the dining room, where Mom was unclogging the vacuum cleaner. I was at one end of the dining room table, carefully taping together my used piano books. We both stopped and cried out. That sudden, sinking feeling was abrasively real!

What was he saying? Can this even be happening?

Those were the thoughts swimming through my head as a little girl, just eight years old.

It was January 7, 1969. Earlier that evening, my dad and I went ice skating. He did his impressive sailor's jig, as he often had before, wearing his sharp, black figure skates. Many kids gathered around him, watching intently as my dad wowed them all with his fancy footwork while outdoors on the local ice skating rink.

He drove me home, parked near the back porch door, where

I stepped out of the car, and walked around to his window. He reached through the window to kiss me good night and tell me he loved me as only Daddy would do. That would be the last time I would ever see him alive. Two hours later, he was gone.

I will always remember the frigid January evening in the funeral home. It was the first time I stood by a casket to comfort people as they walked up to view my dad's body. The first time I would offer hugs and a kind word as they shed tears over losing a cousin or best friend. The first time I wouldn't have my daddy's arms to hold me when I felt afraid. The first time I'd see Mom only with our pastor in a prayer circle. Those hours seemed to drag on and on, but I clearly remember reaching down to touch my dad's face in hopes he would wake up one last time.

My father served in the Army during World War II. At the close of his funeral, I thought of just how brave and courageous those soldiers had been in war. Here they were dressed in their perfect dress blues, standing over the casket and folding a large American flag. Together in perfect rhythm and poise, they handed this exquisitely folded flag to my mom to accept while all of us kids sat next to her watching. It was a somber moment as we looked at each other with tears rolling down our cheeks, embracing each other, one tear-filled hug at a time. This was the first I had seen Mom cry since the night of Dad's death.

I can still see that packed church with mostly familiar faces everywhere. So much love and care for our family was shared and beautifully expressed, yet the confusion was real.

I can still see and smell my dad's black shoes as Mom packed each pair neatly in the donation box along with his button-down shirts and work trousers. My heart was heavy with the reality that he was never coming home again.

Why had this happened? Was God mad at me?

Everything changed from that moment forward.

What seemed like chaos and confusion for many cold, winter days eventually made its way to a more comforting pace as Mom assured me Daddy was in heaven and we'd all be together again someday. My thoughts often drifted back to my dad and the special times we had together.

I remember whispering the Bible verse John 3:16 and trying to make sense of where my life was going. Memories of our family devotions would pop into my head in the evenings when I was trying to fall asleep. My dad would always lead with all five of us kids gathered in the living room. Every night we had devotions, a reading from the Bible, and prayer—even if friends were sleeping over. They would also join our family, kneeling in prayer, all scattered about the living room.

One beautiful, fall night before Daddy died, my mom and I got on our knees, bowed our heads, and closed our eyes. As the wind whispered in through Mom's bedroom window, she put her arm around me and led me through accepting Jesus Christ into my heart. I simply repeated after her a short but life-changing prayer. I was six years old, and I wanted Jesus to be in my heart more than anything. I knew from the many Bible stories I had heard that Jesus gave his Son for me so I could live forever in heaven with Jesus and my family. I just had to invite him in. When we stepped out of the bedroom to share with Dad, I remember his excitement as he picked me up, hugged me tight, and spoke out words of assurance and excitement. It was truly a beautiful reason to celebrate. I'm forever grateful for that night.

My mom carried herself in such a humble, strong, confident, and courageous way, trusting our lives into God's loving care, fully believing we would all be okay. She remained steady, positive, and strong while going through the sudden loss of Dad and all the many changes with five kids, moving, and changing careers. She remained faithful to God, both in prayer and action. I would wake many nights in her bed in horror as crazy nightmares startled me. Mom would comfort me, sometimes sing to me, and always pray over me. Then she would quietly walk out, leaving on a night light. She truly was my hero.

The hardest part took place when my mom announced that we were moving to Minneapolis. Just her and me. She had accepted a position at a Bible college. The move happened, and the settling-in began. Having a blast with my new friends in the neighborhood, within the first twenty-four hours, I found myself in the emergency room with a concussion from getting bucked off my new friend's Shetland pony. Thankfully, these few friends and I stuck together all throughout the next few years of school.

Mom placed me in a private school there. For the next two years, I cried myself to sleep, sinking deeper into a place of despair. The kids were cruel, and I would find a way to become invisible. For days on end, I'd feel lonely, insecure, made fun of, angry, and lost. What was I doing here?

Two years of what felt like a really bad dream finally ended when I entered the local public junior high. My mother was working at a college, where we lived in a dormitory with college kids everywhere, instead of my sisters. It seemed like Mom was always tending to one of those college kids—not me. Desperately missing my life as I knew it, my attitude, choices, and activities didn't line up with what I was taught. Lying became a game, all wrapped up in the excitement of what I could get away with and how not to get caught, which included stealing and cheating repeatedly. This pattern soon became my way of life.

During high school, my rebelliousness and poor choices progressed. My lack of respect, selfishness, need to fit in, and minimal direction all added up to a season of turmoil, desperation, and insecurity. My self-sabotaging lifestyle carried with it plenty of heartache and pain. Mom remained caring and loving to the best of her ability, even though my actions were harming our relationship.

I can look back now and know for certain that my longing for love, acceptance, and attention were all being met in the wrong places. Mom and I moved to a new apartment that had a swimming pool, a private party room, and a diverse bunch of neighbors. I babysat for several couples who introduced me to alcohol and drugs and a sexually immoral lifestyle. I even watched a man's kids while he had sex with my girlfriend. Then there was a single, older guy who befriended me in a seemingly trustworthy way. He taught me how to drive, asked me to babysit his large snapping turtle, and eventually gave me the key to his second-floor apartment.

For months, I chose parties my mom would never approve of and lied about my every move. Was I simply adapting or getting lured into a lifestyle I would soon find comfortable? I was seeking to fill that void in my life—that hole in my heart that my dad used to fill.

Thankfully, even with all my struggles, guilt, and shame, God would show himself. His grace and mercy would prevail, and I would feel his love somewhere in the deepest part of my heart. He really was watching over me.

In my senior year of high school, I received a positive pregnancy test. My boyfriend and a girlfriend took me to Planned Parenthood, where the positive test was confirmed. I looked at them sternly and said, "I'm done smoking, and I'm choosing life! There's no other option!" (I was grateful for my upbringing and my faith in God on this topic.) They were both 100% supportive of me.

I knew God's hand was in this decision. Eight months later, my handsome son was born. Three months later, my boyfriend and I married. We lived in a small town in Minnesota, both working, with our son in daycare and our marriage on the rocks. Less than two years later, our lives were blessed with a beautiful baby girl. We loved our children deeply, but sadly, three years after our daughter was born, we threw in the towel and divorced.

At the first wedding I attended after our divorce, I learned that the friend I met after moving to Minneapolis, the one whose pony threw me, had died of a brutal drug overdose. I was devastated and angry. How could this happen?

Living alone, as a single mom with two kids, and working two jobs, I continued making questionable choices while the kids were with their dad. My party life increased. I became less responsible, and my love for myself diminished with shame, guilt, and restlessness. Obsessed with thoughts about this friend and the sudden loss of both her and my dad, my drinking took on a new role—relief from pain—numbing those feelings I didn't like.

Not long after this, I had a spiritual awakening of sorts. I had prayed and cried out to God for help and, in the midst of this plea, felt the overwhelming desire to quit smoking.

Three months later, one of my sisters introduced me to my next husband on a blind date. Five months later, we were married. He gained a wife and two kids when we moved in with him and began our life in another small town. I really believed this was an answer from God, a gift of hope, and a huge blessing. I was no longer supporting my family on my own, and I had a husband again.

We faithfully attended church, my husband earned a Master of Divinity degree, and we moved to Wisconsin, where we began a ministry in a small country church. Together, we had two more children. So with a blended family, my first ministry assignment, and another move, life presented itself with numerous challenges.

We had limited resources, and once again, I found comfort in the bottle. My duties within the church grew, as did my responsibilities at home. I returned to smoking and drinking once the kids were in bed each evening. This was my repeated comfortable escape.

Soon we were fired, but another church assignment followed. We moved again, this time to a city where, finally, my secrets were exposed.

Suffering from suicidal thoughts, hormone imbalance, headaches, overpowering guilt, shame, and deep restlessness, I found myself in a hospital for evaluation. This was when I was diagnosed as an alcoholic. Blessed by this wise doctor, he strongly recommended I find an Alcoholics Anonymous (AA) home group to connect with regularly and spend a few months in outpatient treatment.

I chose a local AA meeting in a church. Scared out of my mind to enter that room on that barely sober Friday night, I was surrounded by friendly faces, kind, accepting, and welcoming. These new loving friends were telling familiar stories as they took turns around the table. Blackouts, morning regrets, hiding the booze, crazy unmanageability at home, and so much more. Had I really found my people? They would talk about a God of their understanding, surrendering to his will and doing a thorough moral inventory. They would also talk about these twelve steps and suggested I work them in the order they're written. I was excited I might be onto something, thanks to my doctor.

After a few weekly meetings, I asked a woman with years of sobriety to be my sponsor and began working through the twelve steps of recovery with her. I had surrendered, asked God for help, and was willing!

This was the time in my life when I first heard phrases like:

"Clean up your side of the street."

"Do the next right thing."

"You're only as sick as your secrets."

"Relax, take it easy, and the answer will come."

"Our experience can benefit others."

"Self-seeking will slip away."

"Ask God's forgiveness and inquire what corrective measures should be taken."

They even suggested I surrender to God's will. Having never completely lost my faith or trust in God, this was a comforting idea. I began to connect a few of the dots and glean slight snippets of hope, acceptance, and forgiveness.

Have you ever wanted something so bad you'd do anything to get it? I desperately wanted this amazing feeling I was starting to experience to continue. The promises of AA are about knowing a new freedom and a new happiness. I still had doubts, but as my perspective changed little by little—thanks to friends believing in me when I couldn't believe in myself—my faith took on a new direction. It gave me a confident, calm and lasting peacefulness with hope in the promises of my heavenly Father.

In my early journey of sobriety, when I was a year and a half sober, I decided I could do it on my own. Unfortunately, I went back to drinking for over a year. By the grace of God, he directed me back to AA and helped me make the choice to seek sobriety again. I was all in. I had a new commitment and passion in my belly to stay clean and help others on their journey. Knowing God had been working on me and preparing my heart, I was baptized on Easter Sunday morning in 2019.

We have a saying in AA: "You can't keep it until you give it away." This has probably saved my life. Service work is a big part of the twelve steps of recovery. By the grace of God, not only do I have my sober family, but I have also found a community of healthy-minded individuals who take their health seriously with simple solutions centered around plant-based foods.

Today, I am happily married. I have gained a stepson, and together we have five adult kids. Three are married and we have three grandsons.

I now have sixteen years of sobriety, I'm staying true to myself, and am trusting and believing in God's mighty promises. I have faith my marriage will take me all the way with my husband at my side. We have an anchor in Jesus Christ, and our foundation is His Word.

I am Janet Myking Otto, a born-again believer and lover of Jesus. I am faithful and loyal to my husband and continue to take steps as life presents opportunities every day!

Praise be to God!

Amen.

"For the Lord your God is living among you. He is a mighty savior. He will take delight in you with gladness. With his love, he will calm all your fears. He will rejoice over you with joyful songs."

— ZEPHANIAH 3:17 (NLT)

My Cup Runneth Over

By SARA WALTON

I WAS BORN to older parents in Magnolia, Arkansas, in 1952. My family moved to Memphis, Tennessee, when I was three years old. Being the youngest of four siblings, I was raised more like a grandchild, and for the first ten years of my life, I was spoiled.

For as long as I can remember, my family was part of a church but not very active in our faith. There would be blessings were said at the dinner table but only on holidays like Easter, Mother's Day, Thanksgiving, and Christmas. I don't ever remember seeing a Bible being used by my parents or my legal guardians. I do remember going to Sunday school, Vacation Bible School, and church camp in fifth or sixth grade.

When I was just ten years old, my mother died of cancer. I knew she was sick, but no one had tried to prepare me for her death. I remember being very confused.

I was a "Daddy's girl," but my father was an alcoholic and couldn't be trusted to take good care of me after my mother died. My brother, Robert, and his wife, Joyce, promised my mother they would raise me, and they did just that. I left my home and my neighborhood friends to go live with them and their two-year-old daughter, Melissa. My brother and sister-in-law were about twenty-three years old, with a two-year-old and now a ten-year-old in their home. I went from being the spoiled baby in a family of four to being the big sister.

My brother and sister-in-law welcomed me into their home. They accepted the challenge with grace and, I believe, tried hard to see that my childhood would be as normal as possible. Many changes occurred from moving across town, leaving my friends, dealing with my grief, and accepting my new life. I would see my daddy but not very often. When my father suddenly died two years later from an alcohol-related issue, their sweet commitment continued, and I knew I was loved. Melissa, my niece, was now like my little sister. My big brother had always been my hero, and now he was my dad too. I felt safe, accepted, and loved.

My sister-in-law expected good manners from me and encouraged me to always help others. She did her best to teach me many life skills in homemaking and personal care. Good grammar was at the top of her list! Joyce was a wonderful example of a good wife, mother, homemaker, and a strong Christian. I am so grateful to her and love her deeply.

My high school years were fun! I attended a very small high school in Mississippi. I was never a good student and would just get by in most of my classes. I loved the social part of school as well as clubs and boys! My brother and sister-in-law were fairly strict with me, and I was a pretty good kid—never smoking or drinking. I never had my own car, but my brother wanted me to learn how to drive a stick shift so that "if I ever got off with some boy and he started drinking, I could get myself back home." Our family was thrilled when, in my senior year of high school, Joyce and Robert had another baby girl, Emily Claire.

After graduation, I managed to get accepted to Delta State College in Cleveland, Mississippi. On the first day, after unpacking in the dorm, a girlfriend from my high school who lived down the hall asked me to join her, her boyfriend, and his roommate to ride around town. This is when I met my future husband, Steve Walton. We hit it off and were dating exclusively within a few months.

Steve and I married after he graduated from Delta State. I was twenty-one and he was twenty-three. We had a sweet, small, traditional church wedding. I had found a man of integrity who loved his family, wanted to work hard, and made me laugh. This guy was very much like my brother, and that was what I wanted.

Steve and I were not interested in attending church until after our first daughter, Ashley, was born. We were invited by a neighbor to try a new church in Peachtree City, Georgia, where we lived then. I became very active. Steve, not so much. I loved the church community, helping with the children, and being part of leadership. I "played church" for many years, but I didn't know Jesus as my personal Lord and Savior. I thought going to church and signing up to help would get me to heaven. I thank the Lord for patiently waiting for me.

Steve and I went on to have our second daughter, Amanda. Our life was good. We were so blessed with a beautiful home, vacations, healthy girls, great friends, and a wonderful marriage. His job took us out to California for four years. The first year, I was miserable and lonely, but Jesus knew what I was missing and longing for. He put people in my life who helped me grow in my faith and taught me to pray. He gave me opportunities to lead and serve others. The closer I drew to Christ, the more my spiritual gifts became apparent to me. Gratitude became a daily focus in my prayer life. I could see where, in my thirty-six years, God had provided just what I needed and when I needed it. I began praying that my husband would come alongside me.

When we returned to Georgia in 1989, I was excited to return to the church where I had just "played a part" in years past. I was hungry for Bible study, prayer partners, and opportunities to serve. I became a Stephen Minister, where I built deep, faith-based relationships. I led a Bible study and a small group and worked in the women's ministry. I had great Christian women in my life. I prayed every day for my girls and husband to join me. Sports, friends, and work got in the way for them most of the time, but I kept praying.

One of the hardest times of my life was when my precious brother Robert, my hero, was diagnosed with a brain tumor. He was only fifty-six and was healthy in every other way. He lived eighteen months after the surgery and radiation. I traveled over to Mississippi every other week during his last days to help with his home hospice care. I considered this a privilege as he had always taken care of me, and I was with him when he passed away. A huge piece of my heart was lost that morning, and I will never get that back.

When our church was promoting small group ministry, I volunteered Steve and me to host and lead one in our home once a month. Steve saw other men sharing their lives, their God stories, and praying. He really enjoyed being with these Christian couples. God started working on his heart. I began to have hope that Steve's faith would grow deep.

Our daughters graduated from high school and college. Amanda and her fiancé began to attend church during their last year of college at Florida State University. After their wedding, they attended a spiritual retreat called Walk to Emmaus. They insisted that Steve and I attend the next time it was offered, and they would be our sponsors. My husband was reluctant: only a daughter's persistence got him there.

My husband returned home from that retreat a different person. Although he was always a very good man, his heart had been changed. He was now a man of God. This changed our marriage and our family's life for the better. He became our spiritual leader. God hears our prayers! Praise the Lord!

"My cup runneth over" is how I describe my life currently. I have two married daughters, two Jesus-loving sons-in-law, and six grandchildren who are being raised to know Jesus! Seven years ago, I was diagnosed with multiple myeloma, a blood cancer for which there is no cure. Jesus has kept me in the very first and lowest stage of this cancer. I am not on drugs or treatment of any kind.

I am so blessed to serve with The I-58 Mission, a ministry that serves the oppressed, the poor, and the needy. I am able to give back to others as Isaiah 58:6-12 instructs us to do, and I find my purpose there.

I am full of gratitude to my Lord for placing people in my life that I needed as a child, a young mother, and now, as a retired grandmother. I am thankful for the different opportunities I have had and continue to have to help others using the gifts He gave me. I pray each morning that I might find JOY in the new day and that God allows me to scatter that joy to others.

Romans 12:12 describes my life. I am not a person who dwells on the past. I try to be joyful and find the positive in each situation.

I have to be patient in my affliction of multiple myeloma. And, I am ever faithful in praying for others and in my opportunities to serve others.

I hope and pray that my Story of Hope will encourage you today.

"Be joyful in hope, patient in affliction, faithful in prayer"
—ROMANS 12:12 (NIV)

It's A Journey

By PATTI LARSON

1963 TO THE PRESENT

Growing up in an alcoholic, dysfunctional family opens up a person to all kinds of obstacles and choices. Experiencing emotional, physical, and sexual abuse from childhood into adulthood, I made poor decisions, which put me in all kinds of compromising situations.

I married at nineteen and became a mother four months later. I had three kids by my early thirties and a marriage, like most, with ups and downs. My husband's job was very demanding and time-consuming with traveling, meetings, and responsibilities as he climbed the executive ladder and moved us all over the country. This left me with the full responsibilities of raising the family and running the household, which I enjoyed. There were many good times and challenging times trying to navigate my roles as an executive's wife and mother of three great kids.

SUMMER OF 1988

Just when I thought things were mellowing out and I could breathe, my mother died of bone cancer. Mom's life was quite turbulent; she found peace and comfort in the outdoors with the wildlife and in becoming a master Japanese gardener and an artist. She shared her love of gardening and the tricks she learned along the way with me, which I still practice and share with my kids and grandkids who are curious enough to listen and watch.

Working with nature brings such peace. I feel closer to God when spending time with those beautiful gifts. When I am observant and willing to stop and look up, I see his glory. I also have great respect for the amazing wildlife nearby.

Six weeks after my mom's death, our twenty-two-year-old son, Marc, died in a motorcycle accident on his way home from work. Life turned upside down! That's when things came to a halt for me. I had just lost a person who gave me so much joy. He always had a way of making things fun when those around us were so serious. Life is too short to be serious all the time!

I was ready to call it a day—literally. God gave me the choice! At least, that's what I thought He was saying to me at the time. There was nothing wrong with me except that my heart was broken. God let me go through what it felt like to just stop breathing and die. I was not ready, and God knew that, but I had to ask God to save me and let me live. After that, I knew I could survive anything, not realizing the many ways that would be tested.

My son had a fiancée who had gone back to Oregon so they could get their finances in order before marriage. When he died, she came for the funeral and went back to Washington to start over. She eventually married and had a family who are still a part of our family today.

The challenges were not over, as my family often chose chemical dependency to soothe their pain. Having grown up surrounded by this problem and feeling I would also be like that, I said to God, "Okay, if I am going to be addicted to something, please let it be chocolate! It can't hurt anyone, cause a wreck, or destroy a relationship." I can, however, get zits and get fat, but I won't hurt anyone else. So, be careful what you ask for because that is what has happened!

God helped me find a Bible study group through our church, and I sat next to a woman who became like a sister and was a prayer partner throughout my life. We began praying for our broken families and we continue to pray for them to this day.

JANUARY 3, 1993

My husband became unfaithful to soothe his pain. His stressful job, and living a double life, coupled with substance abuse, took a toll. Two months after his fiftieth birthday, just as we were trying to get help and heal our relationship, he died of a massive heart attack. We had been married for thirty-four years. I felt abandoned and devastated, but God reminded me that He wasn't finished with me yet.

TIME TO START OVER ...

As my family grew, challenges continued with brief respites. My surviving children became single parents and got into their own dysfunctional relationships. I tried to surround myself, them, and their children with positive messages and activities, respect for people's things, and signs like "Never quit" and "Smile at the mistakes you survive!" It became a lot.

Many times I would yell at God, "Enough already!" I was frustrated and tired of always being the one to fix things. I wanted to run away and I behaved badly! But when God creates in you a desire to always give life and others your best shot, He provides ways to put you to the test.

As I age and watch the kids and grandkids growing up and see the abuses some of them have overcome, it saddens me that they have felt the sting and rejection of the ones who are supposed to love and protect them. But I also see the beauty and courage emerge as they escape those hardships and choose to make the most of new opportunities.

We can move beyond those who mean to bring harm and destroy our spirits. In *Codependent No More,* Melodie Beattie writes, "We refuse to participate in this any further!" Then we turn and walk away.

THINGS TO REMEMBER

1. Give each day your best.

2. Focus on being a blessing whenever and wherever we get the opportunity.

3. Pray and ask God into your circumstances.

APRIL 1999

My brother had lived with my father in Washington State since my mother's death in 1988. Their relationship was distant at best. At my father's advanced age, this was not good for him. I went back to Washington for a few months to assist in the sale of Dad's home, resettled my brother north of Spokane, and packed and moved Dad to Georgia. On the trip back to Georgia, we checked off a few things on Dad's bucket list, like seeing old friends, visiting the beautiful Oregon coast, and enjoying the amazing seafood there.

We arrived in Georgia in June, got Dad set up with medical aid, and tried to make him comfortable. Through the ministry of dear friends of ours, Dad accepted Christ at the age of ninety, and he went to be with the Lord in September of that same year. He was a smart man with a sparkle in his eyes, a quick wit, and a wonderful family historian. Friends and family alike all have humorous stories about my dad. We miss him.

FROM THEN TO NOW - 2023

I am now eighty years old. I am blessed with good health, an inquisitive mind, determination, and strength like someone far younger. God has given me all that and a wonderful family—a special man who loves me as I do him, friends who I call brothers and sisters, and their families who think of me as family and allow me into their special moments.

LESSONS LEARNED OVER THE YEARS

• Love is indispensable! Put 1 Corinthians 13:4-8 into practice.

• Being a blessing to others takes the focus off ourselves.

• Always be on the lookout for ways to help because more hands lighten the load. There is always something that needs to be taken out, brought in, or put away.

• Be generous with your God-given skills and gifts because God loves a generous spirit. Without God, we wouldn't have anything!

• Be generous when someone needs a hug or a listening ear.

• Be grateful always for the kindnesses shown to you.

• Stop expecting others to fix things you can do yourself or learn to do. It feels amazing!

• Let go and let God is my mantra!

Growing up, I felt like a victim of my circumstances. Now I feel victorious for overcoming those circumstances. It was only by God's grace! Beauty from ashes!

"For I know the plans I have for you," declares the Lord, "
plans to prosper you and not to harm you, plans to give you hope and a
future. Then you will call on me and come and pray to me, and I will
listen to you. You will seek me and find me when you seek me with all
your heart. I will be found by you," declares the Lord, "and will bring you
back from captivity. I will gather you from all the nations and places
where I have banished you," declares the Lord, "and will bring you
back to the place from which I carried you into exile."
— JEREMIAH 29:11-14 (NIV)

Fighting for Joy

By **JOYCE BEVERLY**

I CAN'T REMEMBER WHEN I DIDN'T KNOW WHO JESUS IS.

I knew him before I taught myself to read using the large family Bible on my parent's coffee table. Once I knew my letters and sounds, I read phonetically, my mother helping me by filling in the "big" words. I don't know for sure how old I was, but it was well before I started school. I'm guessing age four.

I have loved words, stories, and books ever since. I knew I wanted to be a writer when I was ten years old.

I don't remember when I first loved Jesus, but it was also when I was very young. I talked to him all the time when I was a kid. I can remember praying randomly while playing and after going to bed at night. I professed my belief in him and was saved often because we usually attended churches where you walked a tightrope over eternity. Backsliding was a favorite topic of most of the sermons I heard growing up. Down the street, the Baptists talked a lot about the security of the believer. It really confused me.

When I was in ninth grade, I fell in love with journalism.

My English teacher recruited me to work on our high school newspaper and set me on a path for a career that followed me for the rest of my life.

I went to camp meetings in the summers between the eighth and tenth grades and probably made a profession of faith again. At about the same time, since the people I loved and trusted most were convinced I could lose my salvation, I decided the Baptists must be wrong. I knew, though, that I could never live a sinless life. I had a lot of energy, a smart mouth, and plenty of faults. I would never be able to stay up to date on all the repenting my temperament required to keep my salvation. So, around fifteen years old, I gave up.

The timing could not have been worse. I battled depression from the time I reached puberty. Serious, can't-get-out-of-bed-sometimes depression. The kind that will land you in a psychiatric ward or hospital. I dealt with all of the angst and confusion by alternating between achievement and partying from age sixteen until I married a handsome guy who represented adventure and security. I left college and followed him across the country when I was nineteen.

At age twenty-one, I searched for the Jesus I knew loved me and found him in a small Baptist church in Arkansas, where my husband was stationed at an Air Force Base and we were expecting our first child. I filled out a visitor's card, and the pastor came to see me a few days later. He took me down the Romans Road and explained salvation to me in a more logical way than I had ever heard it. I reconnected with the Savior I'd known for as long as I could remember and was baptized with a baby bump.

Our son was born five months later. His arrival was the most life-changing thing that ever happened to me. Somehow, I knew that as much as I loved that child, God loved me even more. It was hard to comprehend and yet so precious. A few years later, we had another son. Our first child taught me about love. This one reminded me that my name was Joy.

This may be a good time for a bit of backstory.

My parents married when they were teenagers, the offspring of two families who shared a similar faith but were otherwise very different.

My mother was next to the youngest of twelve children, the granddaughter of a Pentecostal preacher. Her father was a choir director and an entrepreneur. Her mother was an orphan with a sixth-grade education who trusted Jesus when there was no one else she could depend on. I have thirty-one first cousins on that side of the family, and whenever I visited my grandmother, we did not go to bed before she got on her knees and prayed for each one of them, their parents, and anyone else she knew who needed help. It took a while to work through her list. Most of my cousins have this same childhood memory of praying with our grandmother.

My father was the oldest of three, the only son born to another set of teenagers who met at summer camp meeting services just a few miles from where I grew up. In case you're unfamiliar with "camp meeting," it's when people back in the day, primarily from farming communities, uprooted themselves and brought their families along with some livestock and belongings to gather for a couple of weeks of all-day preaching, praying, and singing. It was like a church retreat with the whole family, a milk cow, and maybe your chickens, too.

I'm sure my father's father met the Lord as a child, maybe even at some of these camp meetings, and I know that they reconnected when he was an old man, but in between, he could be difficult.

Certainly, he had his good points, but I am thankful I did not grow up in his house. My father's mother, on the other hand, was a kind woman, but she was filled with fear and anxiety. They doted on me as a young girl, though. I was their first grandchild, and I loved them, especially my grandmother, deeply. It broke my ten-year-old heart when they divorced. Looking back, I think that fracture in our family affected me more than I ever understood.

Mom was nineteen when I was born. Dad was twenty. I was their first child, and they called me "Joy." Officially, I was "Joyce Ann," and some of my cousins on mom's side referred to me by both names. They said "Joyce Ann" really quickly, like it was a two-syllable word in a hurry to get somewhere. If you're Southern, you know that means I'm the real deal. Two first names are the signature of Southern culture. These relatives were a small minority, though. Anyone who grew up with me knew me as "Joy."

Three years after I was born, my parents had a son. Fourteen months after that, another daughter made our family complete. They raised the three of us in a small brick home surrounded by pastures and farmland. The five-mile country road we lived on cut a path through the property of about twenty-five other families whose spiritual backgrounds were very similar to ours. I suspect everyone who lived on that road could trace their Christian heritage back to camp meeting services where my paternal grandparents met.

My parents started off bringing us up in church, and Mom continued after my father lost interest. Church attendance grew sporadic for us, as we were often camping and exploring with our dad.

Once my father realized he didn't have the personality to survive in the structure of a "real job," he launched a series of small businesses, each with great promise but none that succeeded. My dad's circuits were not wired for doing the same thing every day, no matter what it was. Mom went to work as a civilian at an Army base when I was ten years old. Her steadiness and gift for administration kept us afloat.

So I grew up under the influence of two very smart but very different people and became an unusual mixture of opposite natures. I shared my father's adventurous spirit and my mother's need for stability, which makes me a certified anomaly on every personality inventory I've ever taken. I can have a big idea. I can think of more things to do than an army can do, my husband says, but I can also show up dependably to do the same thing every day for years. This simmering stew of nature vs. nurture–DNA vs. environment–means I get up every day with an enormous level of internal conflict.

Let's go back to those teenage party years. When you give up on being a nice girl, you can get into a ton of trouble quickly. Three years is half the length of World War II, plenty of time to lose a war with sin. Decades later, I am still affected by things I chose to do and not to do during this period. I missed very few of the traumas reported by other writers in this book. I take full responsibility for every decision and choice I made, but I am grateful, so grateful, that God sent his only Son to save me. I needed grace as badly as you and anyone you know.

I am also thankful that Baptists never give up on salvation. Whether or not I was falling off a tightrope into the fire of hell before I was baptized at age 21 is a debate for the Calvinists and Arminians. Since then, I've been Baptist, Methodist, non-denominational, and Presbyterian, and now I am Baptist again. I can tell you with certainty that I have tested the promise of forgiveness. A trip to the altar and the baptismal pool doesn't make you perfect, but my experience proves that the shepherd indeed does leave the flock to go and rescue a sheep as often as needed.

Furthermore, I believe that God has protected me from an enemy determined to kill, steal, and destroy me since I was born. I could never list all of the many times I was saved from death, in part because I am sure it happened many times when I was unaware, but I do know of a few very obvious moments.

When I was two years old, I climbed up onto the bathroom counter, opened the medicine cabinet, and ate half a bottle of adult aspirin before my mother discovered me. Neighbors drove us to a hospital more than thirty miles away faster than any ambulance could have made that trip.

When I was six-ish, I climbed up onto my grandfather's truck *(I guess I was a good climber)* and tested the squiggly part verses the straight part on an electrical line to see which would shock me. Only his quick response and a working knowledge of electricity kept us both from dying.

There's no telling how many times I should have died in a car driven too fast or by someone who should not have been driving. No telling.

I struggled on and off with depression until I was in my forties, and still, it taps me on the shoulder every now and then. Mental health issues have killed plenty of people I know, including my first husband. I have no explanation for how I survived except for desperately clinging to Jesus. Whether I was right or wrong, good or bad, a victim or the cause of my own undoing, whenever I asked for help, he answered me.

There's so much more that could be said in every paragraph I've written here. Each is nearly enough for a book of its own, but I can summarize the story with this:

My parents named me Joy. They dedicated me to the Lord when I was just a few weeks old. When I went off course, with death and disaster stalking, the hand of God never left me. He defended me from a powerful enemy I couldn't see.

He replaced my struggle to understand grace with a love so strong I can't deny it.

God kept seeds of faith alive in places where it looked like the ground was barren. He remembered the prayers of a grandmother who asked for protection.

He gave me a second chance with a husband who kept a promise to love me as Christ loved the church. We married under the same tabernacle where generations of my family attended camp meeting services.

He never repossessed the love for words he gave to me as a child. He allows me to help people tell their stories, so here I am pinching myself as I edit and conclude The Women at the Well's first *Stories of Hope*.

He fought for Joy. And he saved her.

And anything he did for me, he will do for you.

If you, Lord, kept a record of sins,
Lord, who could stand? But with you there is forgiveness,
so that we can, with reverence, serve you. I wait for the Lord,
my whole being waits, and in his word I put my hope.
— PSALM 130: 3-5 (NIV)

Acknowledgments

FIRST, FOREMOST, AND FOREVER, we acknowledge our Sovereign God, our creator, and holy Father, the gift of His Son, Jesus, our Savior, and the Holy Spirit, our advocate and teacher, who reminds us of what Jesus said.

"To him who sits on the throne and to the Lamb be praise and honor and glory and power, for ever and ever!"

— REV. 5:13 (NIV)

We are grateful to each of the writers who courageously shared their testimonies in these pages. Each of these brave believers prays for readers to be encouraged by the redemptive power that transforms us.

We appreciate the guidance and talents shared by Joyce Beverly and Cherry Hoffner, editors, and Heather Ward, graphic designer. Their expertise and tenacity are an inspiration.

We appreciate the Board of Directors of The Women at the Well for their compassion and leadership, which nurture the vision and direction of this ministry.

And thank you to all who find hope for the journey in these stories. May you be blessed.

"And we know that in all things God works for the good of those who love him, who have been called according to his purpose."

— ROMANS 8:28 (NIV)

About The Women at the Well

The Women at the Well is a nonprofit ministry that connects women through connection, fellowship, and community. The Women at the Well meets the spiritual, mental, and emotional needs of women with:

- Monthly meetings in which women share their *Stories of HOPE*, from brokenness to transformation to redemption

- An environment of encouragement and authenticity

- Powerful prayer and support

- Hope and faith-based resources for women

- Events, Bible studies, workshops, conferences, and life-changing retreats

Debbie Gronner, Founder and CEO, of The Women at the Well, was called to launch the ministry in November 2016. Debbie is driven to share hope with others as God continues to expand her vision for the ministry.

For more information visit
womenatthewell.us